# Out of Control

# Out of Control

## A CHRISTIAN PARENT'S VICTORIOUS STRUGGLE WITH CHILD ABUSE

## Kathy C. Miller

**WORD BOOKS**
PUBLISHER
WACO, TEXAS

A DIVISION OF
WORD, INCORPORATED

OUT OF CONTROL: A CHRISTIAN PARENT'S VICTORIOUS
STRUGGLE OVER CHILD ABUSE
Copyright © 1984 by Word, Incorporated

Unless otherwise indicated, Scripture quotations are from the
New American Standard Bible, © The Lockman Foundation
1960, 1962, 1963, 1968, 1971, 1972, 1973, 1975, 1977.

Verses marked (TLB) are taken from The Living Bible,
copyright 1971 by Tyndale House Publishers, Wheaton, IL.
Used by permission.

Grateful acknowledgment is expressed for permission to use
material from the following:
    Understanding the Male Temperament, copyright © 1977
    by Tim LaHaye. Published by Fleming H. Revell Company.
    Help! I'm a Parent! by S. Bruce Narramore. Copyright ©
    1972 by the Zondervan Corporation.

**Library of Congress Cataloging in Publication Data**
Miller, Kathy C. (Kathy Collard), 1949–
    Out of control.

    1. Miller, Kathy C. (Kathy Collard), 1949–
2. Christian biography—United States.   3. Child rearing—
Religious aspects—Christianity.   4. Child abuse—Case
studies. I. Title.
BR1725.M447A36   1984      248.8'4      84-7505
ISBN 0-8499-0386-6

*Printed in the United States of America*

To Larry—

my husband, lover, and best friend

# Acknowledgments

I want to thank Virginia Muir whose encouragement at my first writer's conference gave me the original impetus to begin writing a book about child abuse. A year after that, Fritz Ridenour suggested I write my story and this book was begun. Thank you, Fritz!

I also want to acknowledge my friend and neighbor, Patricia LaGraffe, who faithfully prayed for me through each chapter.

I'd like to give credit to my editor, Kathleen Mohr, for her sensitive, careful editing. She made this a better book.

Most of all, my loving gratitude goes to my husband, Larry, who supported me as I wrote, and who encouraged me to share our victorious story.

# Contents

# Foreword

This is a courageous book, written by a brave lady. I say "brave" because it takes the quality of mind and vulnerability of spirit to expose openly one's areas of weakness for all the world to read, especially when that deficiency has been a source of personal embarrassment and condemnation. Some will say that writing a book about such weaknesses is a pronounced act of betrayal against one's own self worth. However, I don't look at it that way.

To me, while Kathy Miller's writing reflects her disproportionate sense of perfectionism with resultant bouts of anger and guilt, that is not the most important message of the book. The message that is written between the lines is of even greater value: Any person who finds him or herself in the human condition—and that's every one of us—is enslaved to a nature and its corresponding emotions which can run wild, take over, or be the guiding force in one's life, until those emotions are recognized, admitted, and confessed to God for His regeneration and correction. Everybody has some hidden "something" which is impossible to disregard or to curb, apart from the strength that Jesus Christ provides as we learn to rely upon Him and His Holy Spirit.

Kathy had the courage to reach out for that hope, and it worked! God met her where she was, and He continues to

meet her as the need arises, because He is true to His
promises and she is willing to believe what He has said.
She has my greatest admiration as a fellow struggler.

I am honored to write the foreword to this book. It is a
very realistic account of one person's willingness to admit her own natural tendencies and find the sufficiency
of power to overcome them in a supernatural way.
And . . . anything supernatural always comes from God.

LUCI SWINDOLL

# Preface

Parenthood. Motherhood. Fatherhood. Oh, what beautiful sounding words those are to an expecting couple. Rarely do they stop to wonder whether or not they have been trained to be good parents. It's not until the dirty diapers, teething cries, and sleepless nights come that the new father or mother cries out, "Where are all the joys of parenthood I heard about?"

I went into motherhood with joy and excitement like many before me. I had heard very little about the negative side of mothering young children. I know now that when I became a mother I had a very naive and idealistic view of parenting. But reality wasn't far behind. And I didn't cope very well with reality. Instead, I reacted with anger, hate, and violence.

I share my story with you, dear reader, in an honest, vulnerable attempt to clear away some of the myths about parental anger and child abuse. My prayer is that this book will provide hope as well as tangible help for those who are struggling with anger. I also pray that this book will help motivate others who are "out of control" to seek the help and support they need. Finally, I hope it will encourage any person to believe that God can help them in their problem, whatever it may be.

The names of some of the people in this book have been changed to protect the privacy of those individuals.

# 1.

## Anger Controlled Me

**March 1st.** Two-year-old, blonde-headed Sandy splashed in the bathtub amid suds and toys.

"Time to wash your hair," I announced.

"No, no, Mommy. No wash hair. Please."

"Oh yes. It's all sticky. It'll feel good to get it nice and clean," I coaxed.

She broke into tears as I rubbed the shampoo into her hair. Suddenly she yelled, "It's in my eyes. It hurts! It hurts!"

"Oh, it is not," I responded. "There're no suds near your eyes. Besides, it's baby shampoo—it doesn't sting."

She screamed louder.

Without warning, I was engulfed with exhaustion. The pressures that had been mounting throughout the day overwhelmed me and I felt weak. The room seemed to close in on me. The dampness and heat made my clothes stick to my skin. Pushing limp hair away from my forehead and gritting my teeth, I hissed back, "Sandy, there's no shampoo in your eyes! Now hold still or you're in big trouble! Hold still, I said!"

Shrieking, she clawed at her eyes. I turned on the faucet and jerked her to it, pushing her whole head under the running water. Soap flowed down over her face into the tub. She sputtered and coughed, but I didn't care. She was going to get clean whether she liked it or not.

I hurriedly turned off the water. Grabbing her arm, I yanked her out of the tub. Sandy stood shivering and crying. I screamed at her again and again. "The next time you'll hold still when I tell you. We'll do it the way I say and that's that."

I felt like an erupting volcano of hate. Anger and frustration boiled inside me like hot lava. At that moment I wanted to kill her.

Spanking her with my hand, I found an outlet for my tension and exhaustion. But spanking became uncontrolled beating until Sandy's hysterical shrieking brought me back to reason. I carried her into her room and dropped her into bed. Slamming the door behind me, I bolted down the hall sobbing.

"Oh, Jesus," I gasped. "I hurt Sandy again. I keep saying I won't do it anymore, but I can't control my anger. What is wrong with me?"

I knelt beside my bed and cried for a long time. Sandy's muffled cries reached me, suffocating me in a blanket of guilt.

My thoughts hurled through my mind like hailstones in a storm. *I've been a Christian for ten years, how can I be so angry? I lead a Bible study and other people think I'm a strong Christian, how can I be acting like this?*

I wanted to scream, "Help me! Help me!" But I was ashamed and frightened. *What if they took my kids away from me? What if everyone knew I was a child abuser?*

*I'm not a child abuser!* I defended myself. *Or am I?*

"I'm still hurting her," I cried out. "I'm abusing my child."

The realization hit me: The title fits. "Oh, God!" The word *abusing* echoed through my mind like a boulder thudding down a canyon wall—strong and final.

There was no hope. I had prayed; I had cried; I had begged for deliverance. If only Larry didn't have to work at night, he could relieve some of the pressure. *How long can I continue like this without seriously injuring Sandy or baby Jeffrey?* Sandy's frightened face flashed before me wrenching my heart like a tree being uprooted by the wind. *I don't want to hurt them. I love them. I want to be the best mother in the world. But I'm so far from that.*

"Oh, Father," I whimpered. "Help me! You've got to. I can't help myself!"

I turned my attention to Sandy and couldn't hear her crying anymore. Walking quietly to her room, I opened the door and peeked in. Her naked body was huddled by the pillow. She saw me and started crying again. Pushing aside my shame, I pulled her pajamas out of her drawer and started to dress her. Her body grew tense at my touch.

"Don't be afraid, Sandy," I said. "I'm not mad at you anymore. Mommy was wrong to hurt you. I'm sorry. I wish I could promise you I'll never get angry with you again— but I can't. Oh, how I wish I could." My tears plopped onto the sheets beside her. I gently tucked her into bed and left the room.

As I put on my nightgown, I wondered if God cared, or if he had deserted me. *Of course not, Kathy,* I chided myself. *You know better than that. God is always there.*

*Then where is the help I need?* I wanted to shout. But I pushed the doubt out of my mind as I cried myself to sleep.

# 2.

# Promises, Promises

**March 10th.** Ignoring Thursday and Friday as they passed, I clung to one anchoring thought of sanity: Saturday would be here soon. Larry had agreed to take care of Sandy and Jeff so I could go clothes shopping. The thought of being out in the *real* world—all by myself for the first time since Jeff was born three months ago—excited me.

Saturday morning finally arrived. As I survived Sandy's temper tantrum at the breakfast table and Jeff's dirty diaper, I looked forward to those few hours of peace and quiet browsing in the mall. Even though several stubborn pounds refused to yield after my pregnancy, I wanted to find a new outfit to enhance my appearance—and boost my spirits.

By the time Larry sleepily walked into the kitchen around ten o'clock, I had verified the checkbook's presence in my purse two different times.

"Good morning, sweetheart," I joyfully greeted him. "You look rested. Your breakfast is on the table and the kids are clean and happy. I'm hoping I'll be back by lunchtime."

Larry's baffled look set off warning bells in my mind.

"Where are you going?"

"Don't you remember? You said I could go clothes shopping today."

"Oh," he muttered. "I forgot. In fact, I don't really remember saying that at all."

"But honey, you said on Monday that this would be a good day for you to take care of the kids."

He still looked bewildered. "I'm sorry, Kathy, but I told Ken we would fly to San Diego today. He's wanted me to take him for a long time and today is the only day he can go. And that Cessna I've been wanting to try out is available at the flying club. I guess you'll just have to go another time."

My throat tensed with disappointment. Despairing thoughts jumbled my words. "But, Larry, you promised. I've been waiting all week for today. I've just got to get out for a while. You don't know what's it's like . . ."

"Well, I'm really sorry, but I promised Ken. You can go shopping any time."

*Any time. Oh sure, any time except when you're flying, or when you're working your "part-time," second job in real estate, or when you need to sleep ten hours a day. Right, any time.*

Angry tears clouded my vision as I furiously wiped the counter. I knew from experience that no matter how long I might continue to debate, the case was closed.

Thirty minutes later when Larry kissed Sandy goodbye, the tenseness in my throat crept into my neck. He shut the back door behind him and my rage surfaced in sobs and cursing. I choked on the apple I was eating and was so infuriated that I hurled it at the door, splattering it over the walls and ceiling.

"Larry," I shouted, "I hate you. I hate you. Can't you see we're dying? Sometimes I wish you wouldn't come back. Your plane can crash for all I care."

Frantically, I stumbled to my bed, knelt on the floor next to it, and cried out my anguish to God. I imagined the scene of Larry's funeral. Friends and relatives told me how brave I was to be so strong. They didn't know that I was delighted in his death. I was free.

"Mommy, Mommy, cartoons are over." Sandy's announcement snapped me out of my self-indulgent reverie, and I slowly pushed myself up knowing Larry's dirty breakfast dishes and Jeff's hungry cry awaited me.

When Larry returned that evening, Sandy's excited greeting drowned my silence.

After tucking the children into bed, I told Larry good night.

"How come you're going to bed so early?"

"I don't feel well. It was a rough day." I hoped he wouldn't press me further. I didn't want to be with him.

"All right. I hope you feel better tomorrow. Good night."

Laying motionless in bed as tears trickled down my cheek and onto my pillow, I wanted to scream my pain at him. *If you really love me, spend more time with me. Choose me instead of your other activities.*

Then I rebuked myself. *That sounds so selfish. I can't say that.*

But the feeling that I wasn't first in his life continued to chip away the foundation of our relationship.

Later, when he quietly pulled the covers back and gently slipped into bed, I pretended to be asleep. However, it wasn't until I heard his steady, deep breathing that I finally relaxed and truly fell asleep.

For the next couple of days I struggled to blow out the flame of my anger and bitterness. But like a trick birthday candle, it rekindled each time I thought about Larry's insensitivity toward my needs. I felt depressed and helpless, as if I were riding a raft down a coursing river without oars or a rope. And my distress calls to God seemed to be unheard.

On Tuesday afternoon after Larry left for work, I loaded Sandy and Jeff into the car and we left to visit my friend Jill. She greeted me at her door, casually dressed in worn jeans and a green turtleneck sweater. Her red-haired, eighteen-month-old son, Aaron, toddled after her.

We settled comfortably on her newly-upholstered plaid couch to watch the news on TV and chat. Aaron and Sandy sat on the floor and scribbled with their crayons as Jeff lay on my lap chewing a rattle.

After a while, the newscaster related a story about a

couple who had been arrested for child abuse. My heart started beating hard and I took a deep breath.

"You know, Jill, sometimes I understand how parents might be tempted to mistreat their children. Kids sure can make parents angry." Laughing nervously, I looked at her and hesitantly waited for her reaction.

"Well, I sure can't," she retorted, shaking her head. "Those people are awful. They ought to be arrested."

I jerked my head away, hot tears stinging my eyes. *Lord, am I really that bad? Doesn't anyone else get angry like I do?*

Gratefully, I heard Jill's phone ring. While she was gone, I composed myself and vowed never to let anyone know how angry I could become. Later when I drove home, I concluded I must not be allowing God to help me in some way. And in an attempt to change, I affirmed my commitment out loud, "Lord, I promise to pray more every day." Yet, I knew my vows had been ineffective in the past. A seed of doubt sprouted within me.

# 3.

# In Training

**March 20th.** Sandy's training pants were wet again! Again! I couldn't believe it. She had messed them only forty-five minutes ago. She had promised she would tell me the next time she needed to use the bathroom.

Marching over to her, I directed her into the bathroom. I struggled to pull down the soaking pants. *What am I doing wrong? I'm afraid she's never going to learn.*

"Sandy, you're supposed to come into the bathroom and use the potty chair. Remember you promised Mommy you would go in the potty chair. Why can't you learn?"

*She's doing it on purpose, I just know it. We've been going through this for several months now. She's done it right before so I know she can do it. She just refuses to obey me.*

"You went potty in your pants. I'll just have to spank you."

"No, no, Mommy. I won't do it again." Her pleading seemed to confirm my speculation.

"From now on you'll go in the potty chair. Do you hear?" Hitting her wet bottom and gritting my teeth, I grumbled, "I am sick and tired of wet pants . . . dirty pants . . . puddles on the carpet . . . loads of extra laundry . . . getting up in the middle of the night to change your soaking sheets."

My tortured thoughts ricocheted in my mind. *You're so*

*much trouble. I can't do anything or go anyplace when I want. You demand love that I don't have. I don't want to be a mother!*

My hands grabbed for her throat. As if I were watching a scene from a murder movie, I saw myself choking Sandy. Her horrified face and fear-paralyzed body somehow satisfied me and I jerked my hands away. But I was terrified when I saw red marks on her neck. Suddenly, Sandy began screaming hysterically.

I ran out of the bathroom. Making my way out the door to the back patio, I pounded my fists into my thighs and cursed myself. "How can I do this again? I've been doing so well. Oh God, please help me. I'm out of control again."

*Maybe I should call someone for help. If I called my pastor, I wonder what his reaction would be. I've never had any kind of therapy before. What would people think of me? How could I tell the ladies in my Bible study that I was going for counseling? They might not respect me any more. They might think God doesn't have the answers. After all, if he hasn't helped me, they'll think he can't help them.*

*No, I'm just going to have to deal with this myself. I know God can help me. I just haven't found the exact answers yet, but I know I'll do better. Maybe if I increase my devotional time and read more Christian books, it will help.*

I could hear Sandy crying in the bathroom. *Oh, thank you, Jesus, that Larry is gone. He just doesn't understand how I can get so angry. I try to tell him, but he can't believe it. I suppose I should be grateful that he doesn't feel anger like I do, but if he did, at least he could sympathize with my feelings.*

Taking a deep breath, I walked back to the bathroom. When Sandy saw me, she backed up to the wall. "It's okay, Sandy. I'm not mad anymore," I tried to reassure her. But when she didn't relax, my heart only felt heavier. I wiped and dried off Sandy and then put another pair of training pants on her. The red marks on her neck were slowly fading.

"Sandy, please remember. The next time you have to go potty, come into the bathroom and use the potty chair. Mommy has a piece of candy for you if you go potty in the potty chair. Mommy doesn't want to get angry with you, but I really think you're ready to be a big girl and wear big girl panties. Then you won't have to wear baby diapers. You can be a big girl with panties like Mommy wears."

Sandy's tear-stained face looked up at me, attempting to smile. "Okay, Mommy, I try."

The next day before Larry left for a business appointment, I asked, "Do you think Sandy's ready to be potty trained?"

"Well, I don't know. How has she been doing?"

"Not very well. At times she manages just fine, but then she'll go for a long time without success. Sometimes I wonder if she wets her pants on purpose."

Larry laughed. "You sound like you think she hates you and wants to get even."

All of a sudden his comment didn't sound so farfetched. "I wonder if I do."

"Oh, come on, Kathy. She's just a little girl."

"No, really. Sometimes when she disobeys me, I think she's doing it on purpose to show me I'm not a good mother. And when she has her temper tantrums, I think I'm a bad mother because I can't make her happy."

"I didn't think you were supposed to make her happy, just obedient."

"But what about the joys of motherhood I always hear about? I'm not a very joyful mother these days."

"Well, I know it's not easy to be a mother, but I don't think you're supposed to be joyful all the time. You're not perfect, you know."

"I guess I'm not. I just want to be."

Larry looked wrapped in thought.

"What are you thinking?" I asked.

He stared at me and said, "I wonder if you want Sandy to be potty trained as early as possible so that your success can be a credit to your mothering?"

At first I started to tell him that his comment was

ridiculous, then I caught myself. "I really hadn't thought of it that way before. I know I don't want to continually change diapers. But maybe I also want her to be a billboard for my mothering accomplishments. Sandy's almost two-and-a-half. I thought for sure she would be trained by now. But maybe she isn't ready. I think I'll give her a few more days and see what happens."

The next few days were disastrous. Instead of getting better, she had more accidents. I wondered if my violent outburst had set her back.

*All right, Lord, I think you're showing me she's not ready, so I'll put her back in diapers. I guess it's better than washing a load of training pants every day.*

Sandy didn't object to being put back in diapers. I was surprised. In fact, she immediately seemed happier and more obedient. *Well,* I thought, *maybe I did the right thing for once in my motherhood career.*

# 4.

# Never on Top

**April 1st.** "Mommy, Mommy, wake up. I'm hungry."

Roused from my peaceful dream world, I wanted to shut out Sandy's insistent plea. *Oh no, not so soon. I was awake nursing Jeff only minutes ago. How many times did he wake up last night . . . three . . . four?* My fogged mind had lost count. I focused my eyes on the digital clock next to the bed, and moaned as I read 5:49.

"Sandy, you can play in your room for awhile. I'm too tired to get up right now. Let Mommy sleep a little longer."

"No. No. I hungry. Come, Mommy, come." She tugged at the sheets.

Larry murmured in his sleep beside me. I knew that no amount of pleading could convince Sandy to leave me alone. Her talking would only wake Larry and he didn't get to sleep until 3:30 A.M. because he had worked overtime.

"Okay, just a second. Let me put on my slippers." Only determination pulled my body out of the warm bed as exhaustion adhesively clung to my muscles.

I stumbled into the kitchen. Dirty dinner dishes lay scattered on the counter, painfully reminding me that I had decided not to wash them the night before. Why had I thought it would be easier to do them this morning? I remembered. I had taken the time to vacuum the carpet instead because it was littered with Sandy's cracker crumbs. I felt better. At least one thing was clean.

I piled greasy dishes into the sink and started cooking oatmeal. I smiled as I remembered that my family's reunion was being held in the mountains tomorrow. Thoughts of sitting outside the cabin in the cool, fresh air, visiting with my family and relatives inspired me to work even faster. Then, out of the corner of my eye, I noticed Sandy running through the family room. Her foot caught on the plant stand sending the philodendron to the floor. Sandy lay sprawled and crying on the floor amidst soil, bits of leaves, and broken pottery.

"My clean carpet! Sandy, look what you've done." Again, anger erupted within me like hot lava.

Gritting my teeth, I grasped Sandy's arms and yanked her to her feet. I felt uptight, ready to explode.

Sandy's chin quivered as she attempted to control her sobs. "Hurt, Mommy. Owee."

A voice within me said, *It was an accident. She's so little.* Suddenly, my heart softened. Unexpectedly, I remembered the last thought I had before I drifted off to sleep the night before: *Lord, I commit tomorrow to you and whatever you might have in store for me.*

"It's all right, Sandy. I know it was an accident," I said while brushing the dirt off her pajamas.

I looked down at the broken pieces of blue pottery littering the floor and started crying. "That's the planter my neighbors gave me when my daddy died. I hope I can glue it together," I sobbed. *Lord, it's just not fair. Not only does it seem like I can't go anywhere, I can't even spend my time in a clean house. Why did I have kids anyway?"*

Vacuuming up the soil, I couldn't control the tears that dribbled down my face. *I am so sick and tired of never having this house clean. There is always something that needs to be done. Before Sandy was born I only needed to spend two or three hours a week cleaning and everything would stay nice for days. Now I spend every day cleaning one mess after another and picking up countless toys along the way. Any time I dreamed of setting aside for myself is consumed by endless loads of laundry and stacks of dirty dishes. I can't put my favorite knickknacks*

*on the coffee table and now, even my favorite planter is
broken!* My self-pitying monologue continued in my mind
until the dirt was gone and breakfast served.

Later that morning, Sandy started sneezing and soon I
was wiping her runny nose. By that evening, her stuffy
nose and hacking cough confirmed my fears: she had a
cold.

"Wouldn't you know it? Wouldn't you just know it?" I
complained to Larry. "We're supposed to leave for the
mountains tomorrow and Sandy gets sick. Why can't the
Lord have a little mercy on me? I want to go to the reunion
so desperately. If Sandy doesn't get any worse I'm going
anyway, no matter what. I just don't care. My fun isn't
going to be spoiled by a sick kid."

But Larry's frown made me realize I couldn't risk con-
taminating everyone else.

Through the night I repeatedly attended to Sandy's
needs. She coughed and coughed and medicine didn't
seem to help. By the time the morning sun arose I had
wearily accepted the fact that Sandy was worse and had
resigned myself to staying home.

*Why is God doing this to me? Is it because of the way I've
been treating Sandy lately? Is he trying to punish me? I
know I deserve to be punished but I have always believed
that my Lord is loving and forgiving. He knows I don't hurt
her on purpose, yet why can't I break my anger habit? I've
seen him work positively in other areas of my life. Why is
this problem so different?*

As the day progressed, I unsuccessfully attempted to
believe God loved me. Physical exhaustion sapped my
emotional strength. I was constantly yelling at Sandy. It
seemed she couldn't do anything right. And when Larry
awoke, I nagged at him too. He left the house earlier than
usual, saying he needed to work on a flight plan.

After Sandy and Jeff went down for their naps at one
o'clock, I gasped at the disarray of the house and began to
straighten up the mess. But eventually I became so weary
that I lay on my bed, convinced that I would rest for just a
few moments before cleaning up some more.

I awoke abruptly and glanced at the clock. *It's 3:05. I can't believe it. Sandy doesn't usually sleep this long. She's not even coughing. Wow, I feel pretty good. But the house . . . Now, I've wasted all that time.*

I threaded my way through the house picking up toys, books, and newspapers. Just removing the clutter made each room look better. I had accomplished something.

*I guess a nap is a good idea. I'll have to take more of them.* "Thank you, Lord, the house looks better."

But my pleased feelings soon surrendered to self-pity as I thought about the fun everyone—except me—was having at the reunion. Through dinner and into the evening my warring thoughts battled for control of my mind.

*The Lord gave me a good afternoon. I got to rest and still picked up the house.*

*Yeah, but why couldn't I go to the mountains? God could have protected Sandy from getting sick.*

*He must have wanted me to stay home for some reason.*

*Yeah, but I could have been a witness for him to my family.*

So on and on the warfare continued.

The next few days I noticed that when a joyful attitude temporarily won a skirmish, I abounded in energy. But when boredom and selfishness reigned, my energy level decreased and depression waved a victory flag.

Several days later as I listened to a Christian radio station, a pastor shared a message about the importance of memorizing God's Word. Of course I had done that in the past, but now I wondered if this could be a part of the solution I needed. My devotions that day covered Psalm 42 and when I read verse 11, I rejoiced. "Why are you in despair, O my soul? And why have you become disturbed within me? Hope in God, for I shall yet praise him, The help of my countenance, and my God."

*This is it. I'll memorize this verse and every time I start to feel discouraged or tired I'll say it.*

Now my inward dialogue turned into praise times. Each time a debilitating thought entered my mind, I repeated the verse. Soon all I had to tell myself was "Hope" and a smile came to my face. In addition, I took a nap every day. Physically and spiritually stronger, now I was able to handle Sandy's sickly disposition during the day and frequent night feedings with Jeff.

My spirit sang. I was on the way to victory. After all, hadn't I passed the test of coping with Sandy's sickness and my exhaustion? It had been more than a week since I had been out of control. I knew I would never hurt Sandy again.

# 5.

# Trusting

**April 15th.** "Larry, Jeff has been sneezing all day. Do you think he's coming down with Sandy's cold?"

"Well, I suppose he certainly could be."

"You know what that means, don't you? We might not be able to go to your parents' house for Easter. We're supposed to leave next week."

"Oh, that's right. And since I'm flying us in the Cessna, we won't have an air-pressurized cabin. That could hurt his ears if he's congested."

Fearful thoughts swirled around in my head. I felt like kicking trust and faith out the door in locked suitcases. *What if we can't go? I'm so looking forward to getting away to Larry's parents' home in the high desert. Even though it's a little more difficult to take care of the kids there, it's nice to visit with Larry's folks and not be responsible for meals and cleaning. I really need to relax there. Larry and I could play tennis at the local high school or take walks in the clear, crisp, evening desert air.*

"Oh, please, Lord, heal Jeff of his cold. I've been good with Sandy and promise to continue. And remember, I didn't get to go to the reunion, so could you please make Jeff better by next week?"

Four-month-old Jeff continued to sneeze and the next day it was difficult for him to nurse because he couldn't breathe through his stuffy nose. Gently stroking his short blonde hair away from his warm forehead, I appealed to God: "Father, I'm believing that you'll make Jeff better soon."

*But if I believe, then why do these nagging doubts harass me like a pesky fly incessantly circling my head?*

"Lord, I'm trying to believe. Help my unbelief."

The next morning, I opened my eyes slowly, surprised that the sun was already up and the house was still quiet. Hadn't Sandy woken up yet? I guessed not. For just a few moments I relaxed as the sunshine ignored the drapes and craftily invaded the room. Larry slept peacefully beside me. I climbed out of bed, went to the window, and turned on the air conditioner's fan. Its steady, dull buzzing would help drown out the morning commotion.

Walking through the quietness, I breathed a sigh of gratefulness. "Thank you, Father. Jeff's congestion hasn't prevented him from sleeping."

But then my apprehension of the previous day resurfaced. *What if Jeff isn't well enough to go in the plane? What if he isn't even well enough for us to drive there?*

I began to fix oatmeal, knowing Sandy would wake up soon, and tried to shove my distrust to a corner of my mind like a child attempting to push down the puppet in a jack-in-the-box.

Only a few minutes later I heard her bedroom door open. She walked sleepily into the kitchen, rubbing her eyes, her faded pink blanket trapped under one arm.

"Hi, sweetheart. Did you sleep well?"

"Mommy, what we do today?"

"It's Monday, so we're going to Bible study. You get to play with the children at Julie's house."

"Goody, goody," she exclaimed as she broke into a little skip.

Hearing that recently-learned phrase made me giggle. Sandy looked so cute as her little round face lit up with excitement. She could be so darling. The ambivalence of my feelings pierced my heart as I realized how much I loved her when she was good and how much I hated her when she disobeyed. But my thoughts were interrupted as the telephone rang. It was Esther, our regular babysitter for the Bible study children. She was sick and wouldn't be able to babysit this morning. I thanked her for calling and hung up. *Oh no, who am I going to get this late? Sometimes I wish I weren't in charge of this Bible study.*

I quickly finished preparing breakfast. *Please, Lord, help me find someone else. I don't want to have to stay with the kids. You know how much I look forward to that Bible study and the Wednesday morning La Leche League meeting. They are my only opportunities to get out of the house. Please!*

The fear of not finding a babysitter and not being able to go to my in-laws' haunted the recesses of my mind as I quickly fed Sandy and dressed Jeff. Sandy jabbered her usual one hundred words per minute, but I didn't seem to hear as I mentally made a list of sitters to call.

"Mommy! Mommy! I want to paint!" Sandy's repetitious whine finally permeated my brooding.

"No, Sandy, you can't paint this morning. We don't have time. I still have to get ready for Bible study and find a babysitter."

"Mommy! I want to paint!" Sandy's insistence grated on my nerves as if someone were scratching their fingernails on a blackboard.

"Sandy," I shouted, "I said no. Now stop your whining!" My jumbled thoughts tumbled over themselves. *Jeff's not getting better. I've got to get a babysitter. I don't want to stay with the children!*

Suddenly Sandy's face turned red. She started screaming and jumping up and down in rage. I grabbed her arm, whirled her around, and hit her bottom hard . . . four, then five times. "You stop that right now!" As I yanked her into the air by one arm, I heard a crack from her shoulder. Yet, I remained angry while I carried her, feet dangling in the air, into her bedroom and pushed her onto the floor. "Now stay there until you can be quiet."

After slamming the bedroom door, I stood trembling in the hall. I listened carefully, fearfully expecting Larry to emerge from our bedroom. But I only heard the humming

of the fan, Sandy's crying, and the exaggerated pounding
of my heart.

I walked to the phone, muttering, "I've got enough to
think about without putting up with her nonsense."

I started calling my list of babysitters but when I had
exhausted it without luck, tears blurred my vision. *I don't
want to spend two and a half hours with those children. I
can't even handle my own. It's almost 9:00, only thirty
more minutes. I guess I don't have any choice now.*

I dressed quickly and ran a comb through my hair. Then
I called Sally, who taught the study, to let her know I
would be taking care of the kids.

"Kathy, just a minute. My mother is here visiting. I'll ask
her to take care of them. She loves children."

"Do you think she would?" The hope in my voice made
me feel guilty so I quickly added, "No, I couldn't ask her to
do that. It wouldn't be fair."

"Oh, it's okay. Hold on, let me go ask her."

My heart beat hard. *Oh, Lord, please make her want to
do it. Please!*

Sally came back on the phone. "Kathy, she says she'll be
glad to. Really, she loves to do things like this. I'll be teaching so she doesn't have anything to do anyway."

I couldn't hide my enthusiasm. "Oh, that's great. I'm so
glad. I'll meet you at Julie's house."

*Thank you, Lord, you did it. I still can't believe it. Thank
you, thank you.*

I rushed to Sandy's room. Sandy, surrounded by her
dolls and toys, looked at me with surprise. "We go now,
Mommy?" she asked.

"Yes, honey, we're going. I'm sorry I got angry with you
earlier. But we have to hurry now." I knelt beside her,
pressing gently on her shoulder. "Has your shoulder been
hurting?"

"No."

I couldn't feel anything wrong, so I quickly dressed her.

A few minutes later at Bible study, as the six of us sat
around Sally's dining room table studying Ephesians, I
continued to thank the Lord that I was there. When it was

time for prayer requests, I asked that they pray for Jeff to recover quickly from his cold. As one of the ladies in the group prayed for him, I felt hopeful, yet doubt still lurked in the back of my mind.

The next day Jeff seemed worse and my faith plummeted like a glider caught in a down-draft.

That week I struggled to build a wall of faith, but I continually allowed examples of God's negative responses to my prayers interfere with my construction. Then I recalled how God had supplied a babysitter for the children at Bible study on the previous Monday morning, and another small wall was erected. Back and forth, the bricks were piled high and then knocked down again. Forgetting to use the mortar of Scripture promises, I appeared to be a clumsy stonemason.

On Friday, Jeff seemed slightly better. He took a long nap and nursed better than he had all week. My hopes soared. I planned what I would pack for the trip to Larry's parents' house.

Saturday morning arrived, and the moment of decision faced us. Larry and I talked it over and finally decided that the remaining congestion was not serious enough to cause Jeff's ears to hurt while in the plane.

As we flew out of the airport Sunday morning, I cautiously nursed Jeff to keep him sucking so his ears would stay clear. During our flight, I reflected on the past week and berated myself for my fluctuating faith. *Lord, all my worrying didn't do a single bit of good. Why couldn't I have just trusted you all along? It was your grace in answer to all the prayers that made Jeff better for this trip. Worrying only made me tense and unhappy and didn't change a thing. I blew it again, didn't I? I lost control with Sandy. When am I ever going to master my anger?*

I looked at Sandy in the back seat. She was asleep. The softened features of her face made her look angelic and peaceful.

*Sandy, I'm sorry. I'm trying. I'm really trying. If I ever injure you, I'll kill myself. I couldn't stand it.*

Tears flowed down my face. I looked out the side window so Larry wouldn't see my grief. The houses and cars below looked small and unimportant. *Lord, is my anger ever going to be an insignificant part of my life? Will I ever be able to look back and see how I controlled it?*

I was afraid to think any further. *I must live one day at a time. Today is Easter Sunday, the day Jesus rose from the dead. I'm going to believe I have resurrected control over my anger and my doubts that will start with this trip. Thank you, Father, that we can go. I know it's a gift from you.*

# 6.

# Bitter Sweet

**April 30th.** As I finished dusting the living room furniture, I turned to Larry and said, "Honey, have you noticed the bills that have stacked up since we got home from visiting your parents? When do you think you'll be able to send them off?" I tried not to sound as uptight as I felt inside.

"Oh, I guess I can do them before I go to work. But I want to finish this article first."

For a moment, I studied Larry relaxing in the blue corduroy lounge chair and reading the magazine that seemed to represent the barrier between us. I pleaded, "Honey, it wouldn't take you more than fifteen minutes to write out those checks. Could you take care of it now, please?"

Glancing up at me, he tartly replied, "Kathy, don't worry about it. I'll do it later."

*Don't worry about it? Doesn't he know how much I hate to see bills accumulate? But I caught myself. I'm not going to nag him. I must trust the Lord. It's not my responsibility anymore. I turned financial matters over to Larry. Now he'll have to deal with the consequences if the bills aren't paid.* Then the thought of paying late charges, when we barely had enough money to cover the bills, began to gnaw at my determination to trust God. I remembered how I used to agonize over paying the bills on time and how I begged Larry to take over the job. When he had finally said

he would, I was glad and so relieved. But now I wondered
if I had done the right thing.

*Father, I don't want to nag him but you aren't motivat-
ing him. Don't you think as Christians we should pay our
bills on time? Please tell him to take care of them!*

As that Monday afternoon passed, I realized it would
soon be time for Larry to leave for work and he still hadn't
made any move toward the desk. I tried to keep busy putting the kids down for their naps and cleaning up the
lunch dishes, but my mind lingered on the obsessive worry of overdue bills.

After he had left for work and I knew he hadn't touched
the checkbook, I fled to the family room. "I'm going to
scream, God. I can't handle it. If I write out those bills
myself, I'll be doing them for the rest of our marriage. I'm
not going to do it. He'll just have to pay the consequences."

I frantically eyed the room. *What can I do to take my
mind off this?* I rushed over to the television and jerked it
on. I flipped the selector around several times and finally
found a soap opera I hadn't watched for several months. I
tried to reassure myself. "Now, I'm not going to get hooked
again. I'll only watch it today. I've got to do something to
get my mind off those unpaid bills."

Within the first fifteen minutes, I became reacquainted
with the plot. Then the first commercial came on advertis-
ing a new cake mix. I nestled among the pillows on the
couch, enjoying the picture of the richly-frosted, devil's-
food cake.

"That sure makes my mouth water!" I tried to think of
any sweets around the house that might satisfy my craving.
I smiled as I remembered the large package of M and M's I
had bought. Rustling through the cupboard, I found it and
returned to my chair just in time to find out that Sue was
on trial for murdering her husband even though Kevin
really had shot him.

By the end of the program, I had finished half the bag of
candy. Scouting the kitchen, I finally decided to hide them
in the potato bin. I knew Larry wouldn't be looking there.

The next morning Candace phoned. She wanted me to

help her start and teach a ladies' Bible study in her neighborhood.

"Wow, Candy, that's great," I exclaimed. "What a wonderful opportunity. How many are interested in coming?"

She explained her plan for the study and then mentioned, "We're going to have it in the afternoon. That's the best time for the ladies to meet."

"Oh. . ." I quietly replied, my shoulders drooping with disappointment.

"What's wrong, Kathy?"

"That just wouldn't work out for me. My kids take their naps then, and there's no way they can miss them. I guess I won't be able to help you."

After I hung up, the sadness in my heart overwhelmed me. "Lord, I want to serve you so badly. I long to reach out and minister to others. Why won't you let me? Why am I stuck home with these children?"

Glancing over at Sandy as she watched "Sesame Street," I could barely keep from darting glances of hate at her. I knew God wanted me to be a loving mother and raise godly children, but somehow it just didn't satisfy me. I remembered the excitement of starting my own neighborhood's Bible study so many years earlier. So many neat things had happened as a result of that study. I wanted to reach out to others again.

*Lord, I want to be used by you like that again. Didn't I write down as one of my goals for this year, "start another Bible study?" Instead of evangelizing the world, all I do is pick up toys, change diapers, and wipe runny noses!*

For the rest of that day, I thought about the candy waiting in the potato bin and tried to determine whether or not Pamela would tell Mark that she was pregnant by Louis.

At three o'clock, I grabbed the M and M's bag and flicked on the television. A load of guilt lay heavy on my heart, but I rationalized, "Well, I don't have anything exciting to do around here, so I might as well see what's happening with them."

The next two weeks were consumed with more and more TV watching and candy eating. The candy filled me up and eventually I only snacked at dinnertime. I was engrossed with the soap opera characters and their problems. At times they seemed more real and important than my own family.

By Friday, my patience level had crumbled. I took the children for our usual early evening walk. When Sandy wouldn't stay out of the street, I grabbed her shoulders and shook her violently. Embarrassed by my behavior, I yanked her into one arm, pushed Jeff in his stroller with the other, and practically ran home.

"Sandy, if you can't obey me, then we won't go for any more walks. One of these days you'll learn to obey me." Feeling my face flush, I slammed the front door behind us.

Sandy screamed, "Walk. Walk. I want a walk."

Suddenly, I realized how tired I was. My muscles felt as if they were attached to one hundred-pound weights. I gazed at the family room. Coloring books, crayons, and bits of crackers littered the room. I wondered how long it had been since I had dusted the furniture. I couldn't remember.

*Now, Kathy, you are really tired—just hang on.* I tried to encourage myself. *Don't let Sandy get to you. In just a few hours both children will be asleep and you will be able to go to bed too.* The thought of the cozy, warm bed made me feel even more exhausted.

The evening dragged. Sandy continued to be keyed up and unhappy. Jeff cried for seemingly no reason. I decided he must be teething.

Finally, after putting them into their beds, I put on my pajamas and slipped between the sheets of my own bed. *Oh, this feels so good. I'm so tired. I hope I'm not getting sick.*

"Father," I began my bedtime prayer, "why does it seem like I never get anything done around here? My house is always a mess, I don't think I'm a very good mother, and I'm too weary to be a good wife. Am I really worth anything? How can you love me?"

My tired body and heavy heart sucked me into a pit of hopelessness. It seemed as if I would never learn the lesson God was trying to teach me. The days merely passed by uneventfully—except for the anger that wrapped a strangling cord around my existence.

*Maybe I just need a good night's sleep. Help me tomorrow, Father . . .* But before the thought was finished, I had drifted into a restless sleep.

# 7.

## Five Gallons

**May 10th.** Jeffrey's hungry cries startled me out of a deep sleep. The sun's rays barely permeated the overcast sky; the high clouds made it seem more like a June morning than one in the middle of May. Dragging myself out of bed, I wondered why I was still so weary. Even after ten hours of sleep, my body felt as though I had just run a marathon.

Plodding through the morning routine, I suspected I was coming down with a cold, but I didn't feel congested. I comforted myself with the promise of a nap.

Jeff went down for his nap easily, but Sandy wouldn't settle down. As I lay down on my bed and started to relax, Sandy wandered into my room, her thin, blonde hair damply matted against her head.

"Sandy, you're supposed to be in bed sleeping. Now, go back to your room."

"Mommy, me not tired. Can I color, please?" Her bright, alert eyes convinced me she really wasn't sleepy.

"Oh, all right. You can color here on the floor while I rest." A warning bell in my brain signaled potential danger, but I assured myself that I would keep an eye on her while I rested.

I got up, found the crayons and coloring book, and spread them out on the carpet beside my bed. Then I strictly cautioned her, "Now remember, Sandy, you color only on the paper and nothing else, okay?"

Her happy face anticipated coloring in her new Lassie coloring book. I smiled, lay back down on the bed, and watched her scribble on the first page.

*Oh, this feels so good.* My muscles relaxed, and as I closed my eyes, I felt peaceful, more peaceful than I had felt in the last couple of weeks. *This feels too good to be true . . .*

Suddenly, I sat up straight. I was still in a daze when I realized that I had drifted off to sleep and had completely lost track of time—and Sandy. Oh no, Sandy had gone. I looked around the room. Half the crayons were scattered about the floor, and the closet door featured quite an assortment of red crayon circles.

"Sandy! Sandy! Where are you?" I implored.

*Oh, no! All the walls will be crayoned.* As I felt a burning flash of anger sear through my body, I wondered whether I was more angry with Sandy or myself.

I ran down the hall, following the crayon-marked walls. Turning the corner to her room, I stared in disbelief as Sandy sat on her bed drawing on the wallpaper.

"Sandy! Look what you've done. You brat, look what you've done! How am I ever going to get all these marks off so that Larry won't know what happened?"

I grabbed Sandy at the shoulders and lifted her into the air. Face to face, I screamed, "Sandy, I told you not to color on the walls. Why won't you behave? Can't you do anything right?"

I shook her. Her head wobbled back and forth as she looked at me in wide-eyed horror. "Brat, brat, brat! Sometimes I hate you."

In my mind's eye, I imagined hurling her onto the floor, her body landing with a dull thud. *I'm going to do it, I want to hurt her.*

A second later, the reality of my thought gripped me. I laid her on the bed. "Oh, God," I sobbed. "I really could have hurt her. *I don't hate her. I hate myself. What am I going to do?*

I threw my arms around Sandy's trembling, whimpering body and hugged her tight. "I'm sorry. I'm sorry. It was my fault you colored on the walls." I coaxed her into my lap and gently rocked back and forth.

"Why am I so irritable and angry, Sandy? I just don't understand it."

As Sandy cried softly, I surveyed all the bad times we had had during the last couple of weeks and one common denominator stood out: the candy! All that candy was making me tired and irritable. My body was reacting to the sugar. In addition, I hadn't been eating nutritious meals.

"Father, thank you. Thank you for showing me. All right, I won't have any more. I promise."

But that afternoon as three o'clock loomed closer, I was haunted by the two candy bars that were hidden in a seldom-used pan in the cupboard. I bargained, "Well, I'll just watch my soap opera and not have any candy. How's that, Lord?"

Before I could hear his answer, I turned on the TV and immediately became engrossed.

As I sat leaning toward the television, I glanced into the living room where Sandy played near a five gallon bottle of drinking water the delivery man had left earlier that morning. *I wonder if she could break that bottle? No, I don't think so, it's awfully heavy. How could she possibly push over such a . . .* But before I finished wondering about the possibility, Sandy pushed on the bottle. With a soft crunching sound, the bottle fell over and broke, spilling five gallons of water onto the green, sculptured carpet. Shocked by the accident, Sandy jumped back, then stared at me in fear.

An overwhelming sensation of surrender flowed through my body as I helplessly watched the water soak into the carpet.

"Yes, I see it, Sandy. It's okay, honey. I'm not going to get angry with you. Mommy wasn't taking good care of you. I finally see how wrong I am."

I turned off the television and began picking up the hundreds of pieces of glass.

"Father, you sure got my attention. I confess that I've been neglecting my family and I've been eating a lot of junk. I ask you to forgive me."

During the next hour, as I used almost every towel in the house to soak up the water, a thought that had been rambling through my mind for the last couple of months surfaced again. *I wonder if my children will grow up and say, "My mother didn't have time for me."*

*Lord, I don't want my children to say that. I really want them to feel like I'm always available and that they are very important to me. I know I complain a lot about being a mother, but actually I want to be a good mother. I don't know why I have such a hard time enjoying what I really want to be. Why do I, Lord?*

Even though no voice answered, I felt peaceful. Sugar and incessant TV watching were no longer going to dominate me and make me irritable. I was determined to spend my time and energy focusing on the Lord. I knew it was going to be different from now on.

Sandy intently watched me spread towels and walk on them to help soak up the water. "Sandy, I promise you that I'm going to try to spend more time playing with you. Would you like that?"

She ran into her room and returned carrying her Candyland game. "Can we play now, Mommy?" she pleaded.

I laughed, enjoying her enthusiasm and sparkle. "Oh, my daughter Sandy, you are a live one. As soon as I finish this, we will play Candyland!"

# 8.

## Big Difference

**May 20th.** "Sandy, I really need to clean the bathroom right now. Mommy is having a Tupperware party tonight, and I have to clean the house. I know I promised last week to play with you more often but today I must concentrate on the house."

Sandy's pout wrenched my heart. Even though I had meant what I said the previous week, each day's busy schedule had pushed aside my good intentions.

"Okay, how about after I finish the bathrooms? I'll stop for a few minutes and we'll play one game of Candyland."

"Okay, Mommy. I get it ready." Her disappointed pout instantly turned into a radiantly happy smile as she skipped off to her room.

By the time I put out fresh towels, I realized how fast the morning was vanishing. I knew I should bake the cake so it would have time to cool before I frosted it. I wondered if I could start it before playing Candyland with Sandy.

*It is such a simple game. Why do I dread playing it?* I knew why. It seemed like every time we almost reached the winning candy house and the end of the game, one of us would draw the lollipop card or the gumdrop card and would be sent back almost to the beginning. Sometimes the game would continue for hours. And the fact that Sandy inevitably folded the cards or threw them around the room also irritated me. I would be glad when she was older and we could play more sophisticated games. But I reminded myself that if I didn't want to play with her now, she probably wouldn't want to play with me then. I feared the consequences of not spending enough time with Sandy in these early years and felt guilty about my selfishness. *Oh, Father, will I ever be the mother I want to be?*

"Well, enough of this," I scolded myself. "I've got to get busy."

I tiptoed into Sandy's bedroom and peeked around the corner. She was carefully laying out the colored cards around the Candyland board.

"Oh, good," I thought. "She's busy so I'll go start the cake."

But I had not even finished combining the ingredients when Sandy ran into the kitchen carrying a handful of Candyland cards. "Mommy, ready to play?" she asked.

"Oh, honey, I'm sorry. I decided to mix this cake first. Can you wait a few more minutes, then we'll play?" I tried to sound cheerful, hoping to ward off a temper tantrum. At first, as her lower lip started to quiver, it seemed that I was going to be unsuccessful. But then the phone rang and distracted her.

"Me get it, me get it," she yelled.

"No, Sandy, only Mommy and Daddy answer the phone."

I watched Sandy out of the corner of my eye as she walked away folding two cards in half. *Oh well, at least she didn't have a fit.*

I picked up the receiver and sadly listened as a friend told me she wouldn't be able to come to the Tupperware party. I felt disappointed but tried to sound understanding as I accepted her apology.

Turning my attention back to the cake, I realized I couldn't hear Sandy. I walked into the living room to check on her and stopped short. She was sitting on the fireplace hearth, sprinkled from head to toe with sand from the gas logs. A thicker layer of the sand encircled her on the bricks and carpet.

"Sandy!" I screamed. "What are you doing? I've told you over and over again to stay out of the fireplace. Just

look what you've done. I'm trying to keep everything clean
for company tonight."

I marched over to her and yanked her to her feet. I spanked her and even though my hand stung, I continued to hit
her again and again. "Damn you. Why can't you do anything right?"

Sandy's screaming egged me on. "Maybe if it hurts
enough, you'll obey me next time."

When I could no longer stand the pain in my hand, I
pushed Sandy down on the couch. Ignoring her sobs, I
jerked the vacuum out of the hall closet, snapped it on, and
furiously pushed it back and forth over the sand. Occasionally I glared at her and lectured, "Why do you continue to do the things that you know make me so mad? I
can't understand it."

Sandy's tear-filled eyes pleaded with me. When my anger subsided and all the sand had been vacuumed up, I sat
down beside her. "Sandy, Mommy has told you before that
you are not to play in the fireplace. I just don't understand
why you keep doing it. I don't want to get angry with you,
but I'm so uptight about getting everything ready. Please
help Mommy by doing what I tell you, all right?"

Sandy rubbed her eyes. I knew I should give her some
attention but the thought of not being ready for the party
made my neck muscles tighten. I rationalized, "I'll get
everything ready for tonight, then I'll have time to play
with you."

For the rest of the day, I cleaned the house, prepared
the refreshments, and kept a close eye on Sandy. Jeff
woke up early from his nap, was fussy from teething, and
needed to be held, so I didn't get everything done as
quickly as I'd hoped. It was five o'clock when I finally
finished. With a sigh of relief, I plopped Sandy on the
floor in front of the television to watch "Sesame Street"
and then fixed dinner.

When only eight people arrived for the Tupperware party, I realized that there had been no reason to get uptight or
angry and regretted that I had spent so much time cleaning
the house, instead of playing with Sandy.

During the following week, Sandy's behavior continued to deteriorate. Every time I started a cleaning project or sat down to nurse Jeff, she found a way to get into trouble. She emptied soil out of the houseplant pots even though I repeatedly spanked her. Her jealousy toward Jeff increased; when she thought I wasn't watching, she pinched him or hit him. Her disobedience was getting worse but it seemed as though I was powerless to stop it. Spankings didn't deter her. I thought she would want to avoid my anger but instead, the struggle for power was intensified—and so did my guilt.

I was convinced my anger was at the root of Sandy's temper tantrums. I kept thinking that if I wouldn't get so angry with her, she wouldn't disobey. The more I thought about it, the more I realized that I was trying to be perfect. For some reason, I believed that if I were perfect, Sandy would be too. *That's ridiculous*, I chided myself. *You'll never be perfect and neither will Sandy.* I knew then that I should work on getting my anger in control but that I shouldn't expect Sandy to always obey me. After all, what child did? Somehow, that realization relieved my mind.

However, I did think I should give Sandy more attention. At times, I knew that I was neglecting to fill her emotional needs. *Why does cleaning the house seem more important than paying attention to Sandy?* I wondered. As I looked around the house, I realized that a neat house gave me tangible proof that I had accomplished something. When I gave Sandy attention, I didn't have any concrete evidence that I had done anything worthwhile. She still disobeyed me! Plus, it was difficult to give Sandy the love and attention she needed because I didn't feel very loved myself.

I longed for the days before Sandy was born, when Larry and I did so much together. Larry had been the companion and best friend I'd always wanted. But now that our lives were so busy, we were growing farther apart and my nagging pleas for Larry's attention only widened the gap between us.

Just as I begged for Larry's attention, Sandy's disobedience pleaded with me, "I need you. I want your attention and approval."

But I could think only of my needs and would respond harshly: "Then why don't you obey me and be a good girl?"

Little did I know that her answer would have been: "Because then you won't pay attention to me at all."

Several weeks later at Bible study, one of the women raved about a book she had just finished reading titled *Help! I'm a Parent* by Dr. Bruce Narramore. I asked her if I could borrow it sometime and she excitedly brought it over that afternoon. By the time I was halfway through it, I could understand how I was failing by punishing Sandy rather than disciplining her.

In the book, Dr. Narramore explained the difference between punishment and discipline. He said punishment is retribution but discipline is training. The focus of punishment is on the past misdeed, whereas discipline focuses on future correct deeds. When he suggested positive use of the phrase, "Mommy will have to spank you so that you will remember not to do that again," I memorized it and practiced saying it over and over again.

As I continued reading, I recognized that I had been inconsistent in my spanking. Sometimes I would spank her for something she did wrong, but other times I would let the misbehavior slide by. For the first time I also realized that my anger was not going to create an obedient spirit in her.

I was excited! I couldn't wait for Sandy to misbehave so that I could try the new disciplinary techniques I had learned. I didn't have to wait long.

The next morning I discovered Sandy playing with the telephone. Just two days before, I had yelled and spanked her for doing the very same thing and here she was, doing it again. Anger started to well up inside me, but I seized control and decided that this was the perfect opportunity to try out my new method of discipline. I took a deep breath, walked over to her, and said, "Sandy, you know that you are not supposed to play with the telephone."

Then, I almost said, "I'm going to spank you because you played with the telephone," but I remembered the phrase I had memorized and instead stated, "Sandy, I am going to have to spank you so that you'll remember not to play with the telephone the next time."

I guided her to her bedroom and told her to stay there. I went to the kitchen and took the wooden spoon out of the drawer. As I walked from the kitchen back to the bedroom, I reminded myself I was training Sandy, not taking revenge for her disobedience. I was surprised at how calm I remained.

When I returned to Sandy's room, she mischieviously grinned at me, probably reasoning that she wasn't in trouble because I wasn't angry. Picking her up and holding her close, I explained again, "Mommy is spanking you because I love you and because I want you to remember not to play with the telephone." I gave her three quick swats across the bottom. She started crying as if she were going to have a temper tantrum, but I continued to hold her close. She stopped crying within two minutes. Blinking back tears, she penitently murmured, "No more telephone, Mommy."

I wanted to jump for joy. I rejoiced, "Oh, thank you, Jesus, this is the way it's supposed to be. I didn't get angry, I didn't spank her too hard."

For the next couple of days I calmly used the spoon each time Sandy disobeyed. Soon, all I had to do was tell Sandy I was going to get the spoon and she would immediately obey.

I was ecstatic. It seemed too good to be true. I was seeing effective results from disciplining Sandy correctly. I congratulated myself, "I'm actually doing something right."

# 9.

## Can't Say No

**May 30th.** "Hi, is Kathy Miller home, please?"

I shifted the telephone receiver to the other ear. "Yes, this is she."

"Hi, Kathy, I'm Ruth from the church office. We're calling to see whether you'd consider teaching one of the preschool Sunday school classes this summer. Our summer session starts in two weeks on June 13th, and lasts until school starts. We'd really love to have you help us."

Hesitating, I grappled for words. "Well, uh . . . Oh, I see. Well . . . I have taught a children's Sunday school class before but that was a long time ago."

"I can understand your concern, but our teaching materials are excellent, and of course, you'd have an assistant to help you."

My thoughts tumbled over each other. *I wonder whether she would be so quick to ask me if she knew I was a child abuser. Considering I can barely cope with my own kids, I wonder how I'd handle the pressure of teaching. But they always need people to help. I really should do my part.*

The gapping pause was awkward. I strained to say something. "Well, I'd like to help because I really appreciate everything my daughter learns in Sunday school. Uh, I guess there's no reason why I can't . . . but I really should talk it over with my husband. How about if I call you back tomorrow?"

"That would be fine. I'll look forward to hearing from you then. Goodbye."

"Goodbye."

I hung up and anxiously faced the reality of knowing what Larry would say. He usually contended that I had too much to do already and should drop some of my activities. I would defend my position and say that I needed opportunities to get out of the house. Certainly, I wasn't looking forward to talking with him about this situation.

As I thought more about teaching the class, I began to wrestle with my feelings of "duty." *Shouldn't you do your part? If Sandy's receiving, you should be giving. If you don't do it, who will?*

Visualizing Sandy's faithful teacher and her happy welcoming smile each Sunday, I wondered if I could find joy in taking care of other children when I didn't even enjoy my own.

The next morning after Larry woke up, I explained, "Larry, one of the ladies from church called yesterday and asked me to teach a children's Sunday school class for the summer months. You know, Sandy learns so much at church, and I want to do my part. What do you think about it? I bet I could handle it. I'm sure it wouldn't take very much time." I hesitantly smiled at him, trying to appear convinced myself.

His eyebrows frowned over his hazel eyes. "Well, I'm not sure you have the time to do it. And even if the preparation time were small, you'd still have the pressure of getting it done. Right now you barely have enough time to keep the house clean."

I could feel a mass of hurt begin to grow within me. "But, Larry, I really feel obligated to help. What if no one helped? Sandy wouldn't be learning more about Jesus."

Larry's grin assured me that he knew I wasn't really convinced myself. "Honey," he pleaded, "you just don't have enough time or energy. You are so busy with Jeff because he's still just a baby. And Sandy is a handful. I'm proud of you for wanting to help, but you'll just have to trust the Lord to supply someone else to fill the gap. He can do it, you know.''

When Larry rose from his chair, I knew the discussion was over. I reluctantly admitted to myself that what he said was true, but guilt overwhelmed me anyway. *Why do I have such a hard time saying no to anyone? That must be the hardest thing for me to do. I've accepted more commitments than I can handle just because I couldn't refuse someone's request.*

For most of that day, I tried to get up the nerve to call Ruth back. Over and over, I rehearsed my lame-sounding excuses. By the end of the day, I still hadn't called. Every time the phone rang, I jumped fearing it might be her.

Shortly after dinner, I discovered Sandy playing with the telephone for the second time that day. "Sandy, I told you earlier you can't play with the telephone. Why do you keep doing it?"

Then it hit me. I had been so uptight about calling Ruth that I hadn't been disciplining Sandy. I'd been giving her all sorts of yelled warnings but no action.

I smiled at her. "Well, little girl, I guess it's time to get back on course again."

The next morning I forced myself to dial the church's number. When Ruth answered, I explained that my husband didn't think I had enough time to fulfill such a responsibility. I falteringly went on to explain that our son was still a baby and required a lot of attention. As I went on and on with all my excuses, I knew I was verbalizing insecurity.

Ruth politely accepted my explanations and said she was sure the Lord would provide someone to teach. I hoped so, but wondered how he could if people like me didn't do their part.

Feeling foolish, I hung up. I rebuked myself, *Your immaturity shows when you can't give a simple explanation or say no. What weak faith you have when you can't trust the Lord to fulfill a need.*

Then I remembered something a friend had shared with me several months earlier. She had learned that "a need is not necessarily a call." At the time she had repeated it to me, the phrase hadn't meant much, but now I mulled over its significance. *If someone expresses a need to me, it doesn't necessarily mean that God intends for me to accept the challenge.*

Even as I sighed in relief, guilt knocked at the back door of my emotions. But I didn't let him in. "No. No! I'm not going to feel guilty again. I've got too much to do now without taking on new responsibilities. I've got to work on controlling my anger," I cried out, trying to convince myself.

As I thought about that phrase during the next couple of days, I realized that if I accepted a project or a position that God didn't want me to assume, I would be taking away an opportunity from the person who God truly intended for the responsibility. I would be robbing them of their blessing.

By accepting such a position I might be able to minister to others, but it could also prevent me from being where God really wanted me to be.

This was starting to take shape in my mind. I didn't have to feel guilty. It was up to God to supply for every need; not me. I was only supposed to do what he wanted me to do; therefore I could say no.

I chuckled to myself as I thought of how often Larry teased me by saying, "Assert yourself!" Now, I knew how I would reply the next time: "NO!"

# 10.

## Church Picnic

**June 8th.** "Larry, have you thought any more about going to the church picnic tomorrow? I really want you to go. It'll be such a great opportunity for us to have a family outing and Sandy is looking forward to it."

Even as I spoke, my soul beseeched, *Please give him a desire to go, Lord.* When I had first mentioned the occasion earlier in the week, he hadn't been sure he'd go. So I had prayed all week that he would change his mind and want to come.

Larry turned away. "Well, it looks like I'm going to have a real estate appointment tomorrow."

"If it's in the morning you could come after you finish," I suggested.

Dropping onto our couch, Larry riveted his eyes on me and explained, "Kathy, I don't want to go. I'm sorry, but it just doesn't sound like something I'd enjoy. You go and have a good time with the kids."

A lump grew in my throat and tears darted into my eyes as my spirits plummeted to the ground.

"Honey," I pleaded, "I just don't understand why you don't want to go with us. Please come. *Please!*"

"Kathy, this isn't the only activity for families, you know. We'll do something together at another time."

I turned and walked out of the room, tears streaming down my face. *Lord, am I so wrong to want us to do things together? Are his real estate deals more important than his family?*

I wanted to bang my fists against heaven's gates, demanding an answer. *Father, why don't you change Larry? Why don't you make him want to spend more time with us? I'm so lonely.*

Larry followed me into the bedroom. I brushed away my tears before he could see them.

"Kathy," he prodded, "are you upset? I promise we'll do something another time."

I wanted to fling abuse at him, to pour out my hurt and let it sting him too, but I felt discouraged. What good would it do? I knew it would only create an unresolved argument.

I began making the bed and in contrived cheerfulness replied, "As much as I want you to go, I can't force you if you think you won't have a good time."

"Thank you." His smile deepened my pain.

The rest of the day I stayed away from Larry. A cage of resentment trapped me inside. Even though I had let myself in and closed the door with a loud metallic clang, the sign outside read, "Courtesy of Larry."

The next morning, the thick-barred cage still enclosed me. But now it was smaller, choking off my ability to forgive. As I hurried around the house attempting to wash several loads of dirty clothes and water my houseplants, Larry wrestled with Sandy on the couch. Her cries of delight irked me. *He gives Sandy so much attention. Why doesn't he give some to me? He says he loves me but he won't even come to the picnic.*

Larry and Sandy's continued roughhousing drove me to keep busy with preparations for the picnic: making a salad, forming the hamburger patties, and packing up diapers and clothes for the children.

When Larry stood ready to leave, he picked up Sandy, hugging and kissing her. Standing nearby, I waited for him to reach over and kiss me. When he walked out the door with only a "Bye, Kath, see you this afternoon," I silently walked away.

"Sandy, come into your bedroom so we can get ready. We only have a few minutes before we must leave." Noticing the pile of unfolded clothes and the dirty breakfast dishes, I felt the wheels within me turn faster. I rushed about in a futile attempt to slow down time.

"Sandy, I said come into your bedroom," I yelled down the hall. She ran into the bedroom, jerked open a drawer, and flung out an old playsuit.

"I want to wear this!" she exclaimed.

I groaned. "But, honey, that is all stained. It's so old I can't get it clean anymore. Look at this nice new outfit I bought you. It has a cute bear on it."

She shook her head back and forth emphatically. Her thin hair whipped across her face, loosening the barrettes I had put in earlier.

"Sandy, stop moving your head so much, your barrettes are going to come out. Now look, you can't wear that. It looks dirty. Come over here right now and I'll put this on you."

Sandy impetuously threw the clothes down on the floor and jumped up and down, screaming. Her crying grated on my nerves. It seemed as if she were saying, "I have a need and you aren't meeting it. You are a bad mother."

When I couldn't stand it any longer, I barked, "Sandy, stop that right now. I'm telling you that you'll wear this outfit. I'm going to get the spoon. Now stop it!"

Thinking I would move past her to get the spoon, I stood up. Suddenly her rebellious, whining cry overpowered me. "You look like your father and you're just as obnoxious," I screamed back at her.

Instead of taking a step, my foot rammed forward, kicking Sandy in the leg. "I can't stand your crying. If you don't stop it right now, I'll kick you again."

Sandy crumpled to the floor, crying out in fear and pain. I grabbed her shoulders hard, hissing, "I'm sick and tired of your temper tantrums and crying. That's all you ever do." I continued to verbally assault her, letting all my frustration and hate pour out.

In an instant, horror replaced my ebbing anger as I realized what I had done. I burst into tears and knelt beside Sandy as she sobbed. *Oh God, what in the world have I done? God, God, where are you? Please help me. I've been doing so well, why can't I cope now? When am I going to be able to control myself?*

Larry's gun flashed through my mind. *I might as well die. I'm no good to anyone, especially Sandy. I'm destroying her . . . and myself.* But I knew that even though misery engulfed me, there had to be an answer other than suicide.

I rubbed Sandy's leg but couldn't feel anything wrong except for a slight bruise. "Sandy, I'm so sorry. I don't know what's wrong with me. I can't seem to help myself. Please don't cry next time. I can't stand it. It tears me apart. I just want to make you happy."

I didn't want to see Sandy's tear-filled face. Avoiding eye contact, I lifted her to her feet, and explained, "We've got to hurry now." I dressed her in the new outfit. She didn't complain.

In a blur of agony, trying not to think, I gathered everything together and packed it in the car. Wiping my tear-covered face as we drove down the street, I tried not to look over at Sandy sitting silently in her car seat.

We arrived at the park and I attempted to smile as friends greeted me. Remaining on the verge of tears, I was panicked that someone might comment about my pained look. I spread a blanket for us to sit on and vaguely noticed the clear blue sky and the warm, leaf-rustling breeze. My depressed spirits contrasted with the beautiful summer California day. Some families around me relaxed or played softball. Others prepared grills for barbecuing. Sandy excitedly ran to the nearby playground while I settled Jeff on the blanket.

I squeezed the last hot tears out of my eyes, embarrassed lest anyone see them. Watching the other families happily playing together or visiting with each other drove a knife through my heart. The struggle within me was a waging war. On the one hand, I wanted to accept Larry as he was, but on the other, I wanted him to be the husband I needed.

I wanted to scream to heaven. *Why isn't Larry here? Doesn't he love me and his family? Sometimes I hate him. For sure, I hate myself and what I've done. I can't ask your forgiveness, Lord, I'm so ashamed. How can I call myself a Christian? I've hurt Sandy so many times, and I'm afraid I'll do it again.*

Hopelessness consumed my icy heart. The breeze warmed my body but not my soul. *Would anyone be sad if I killed myself? I don't think so—not if they knew the real me, the angry me.*

# 11.

## Confession

**June 10th.** Saturday and Sunday passed without my acknowledgment. Sinking in a quagmire of depression, I didn't want to face the fact I was regressing. In fear of hurting Sandy again, I tried to avert any conflicts with Sandy or Larry.

At Bible study on Monday, my friend and co-leader of the Bible study, Sally, briefly commented on my gloominess, but I told her that I didn't feel well. When she invited me over on Wednesday afternoon to talk about our next set of lessons, I apprehensively wondered if she would try to delve into the reasons for my sullenness. But I assured myself that she sincerely wanted to plan for the next session. How thankful I was that she was helping me guide the Bible study until Jeff was older and I could take responsibility for leading it again.

On Wednesday afternoon, with Jeffrey in his stroller and Sandy dressed in shorts on this warm June day, we walked down the block to Sally's house. With each step more fear swelled within me. *She suspects something wrong, I know it. But how could she?* The burden I carried was overwhelming. I suspected everyone looked at me with suspicious stares. A part of me dreaded, yet another part hoped, for a confrontation with Sally.

Dressed in jeans and a tailored blue blouse, Sally answered the door in her usual cheerful manner. I settled in her family room and we chatted as she fixed iced tea. Her bright green eyes sparkled at me, and she smiled with a joy in the Lord that I envied.

I loved to come to Sally's house. I felt peaceful just being there. I could tell she had older children by looking at her immaculate home. Her kitchen counter was clean and neat, and it looked like she had just vacuumed her carpet.

"Well, Kathy," she interrupted my thoughts as she set my glass of tea on the coffee table, "have you thought any more about what we might want to study next session? We've got a couple of weeks to order the materials."

We talked about potential topics, then our conversation drifted to our children after Sally's sons wandered into the room with a balloon. Sandy batted the balloon back and forth with them. Perplexed by the strange yellow floating ball that bounced off his nose, Jeff laughed in delight.

"Kathy," Sally commented, "I've never seen Sandy so animated."

"You're kidding," I laughed. "She always has that much enthusiasm, if not more."

"She must be quite a handful. I remember Shawn had that much energy but Bryan seemed a little calmer. It seems like God usually gives us children with different personalities. Is Jeff calmer or more active than Sandy?"

"Oh, Jeff is definitely calmer. He's my little sweetheart. He's so easy to take care of. I sure wish Sandy were like him. Sometimes I get so upset at Sandy, I could . . ." I stopped. My palms grew wet and clammy. My mind flashed back to Jill's shocked reaction so many months before.

*I can't tell Sally. I'm sure she has never been so angry with her boys that she wanted to kill them.*

My face flushed and I glanced up at Sally. She intently waited for me to finish. "Oh, sometimes Sandy really gets on my nerves," I blurted out.

Sally continued to gaze at me as if I had something more to say. *I wish she wouldn't look at me like that. She won't understand.* But my heart wanted the polluted flood waters, which thrust against my emotional dam, to be released so that the reservoir might be refilled with clean, clear spring water. Stinging tears sprang into my eyes. *But if I don't tell someone, I'm going to explode. I don't want to hurt Sandy again.*

"Well," I hesitantly began, "Sandy gets to me sometimes and I have a hard time controlling my temper. Sometimes I'm afraid I'm going to hurt her. I've taken my anger out on her in some terrible ways."

There, I had said it! The horrible truth was out.

Afraid to confront Sally's condemning look, I glanced the other way. When she started to speak, I cringed inside. *Here it comes. I knew I shouldn't have said anything.*

"Yes, I can remember feeling so angry with Shawn one time that I shook him by the shoulders until his teeth clattered. Those were some very difficult times."

I turned my head toward her, my mouth dropping open. "You're kidding. *You* did that? I wouldn't have thought you'd do something like that."

Sally laughed. "Oh sure, I think most mothers feel that kind of rage at one time or another. I certainly hope I'm not the only one."

"But, but . . . how do you cope? What's your secret?"

"Well, if you mean my formula, I don't have one. Although I have found that when I feel that intense kind of frustration or anger, I try to deal with it in a constructive way."

I sighed with relief. *I'm not the only mother who feels that kind of rage. I'm not alone. Oh, thank you, Jesus. Thank you.*

I wiped the tears from my eyes. *Does she really understand what I've been talking about? Does she realize what I'm telling her? I don't know, but it doesn't matter. She feels strong anger, too!*

"Sally, what are some ways you've found to deal with anger and frustration? I'm really desperate."

Sally's eyes looked distant for a few moments. Finally,

she broke the silence and said, "Well, let's see. I think being aware of when I'm under extra stress helps me to control my anger before it starts to control me. My body often tells me through tense muscles or headaches that I'm too tense. I know then I need to make some changes in my circumstances."

"Yes, I can relate to that," I interrupted her. "Now that you've mentioned your reactions, I realize I have a tendency to grit my teeth when I start to get angry."

"Since you recognize that, try to distract yourself from your anger when you begin to grit your teeth."

"What do you mean when you say, 'distract yourself'?"

"Well, you could pound on a pillow, or do some vigorous exercise like running in place, or even play the piano. Just do *something* to relieve the pressure and give yourself breathing space so you can think about the real cause of your anger. You see, most of the time when I'm angry at my children, I discover that they aren't the true cause of it. It's usually something else that I'm not trusting the Lord for. I really believe that the bottom line of coping with my stress and anger is completely trusting that God is in control of my life—and letting him have his way."

I knew she was right. I wasn't trusting the Lord for my marriage or submitting to his plan for me as a mother. I always blamed the kids for my anger, but actually I was bitter toward Larry and God for my discontent. I felt hesitant to tell Sally about the unhappiness I felt in my marriage, so instead I asked her, "Sally, will you pray for me about this? I'm really afraid I could hurt Sandy. I've prayed about it for a long time by myself, but I can't seem to get control. Maybe if you pray with me, the Lord will perform a miracle."

Sally nodded. "Of course, I'll pray for you. I'll pray every day that the Lord will reveal what the root of the problem is so that you can dig it out and expose it. And remember, don't be too hard on yourself. God knows you can't be perfect here on earth, so don't expect that of yourself. Only Jesus is perfect. We're still in the process of growing. When you feel really uptight or angry, give me a call and we'll talk about it."

I thanked her. As we talked for a few minutes longer, I felt like bursting with joy. I had revealed my horrible secret and she hadn't condemned me or even reacted with shock. She understood! She still respected me as a person and as a Christian. Would her support and prayers be the answer? I hoped so. How I wanted this to be the end of my awful nightmare.

During the next few days and into the weekend, the burden of my anger was gone. I remembered to discipline Sandy consistently and whenever I sensed I was tired, I took a nap. Sometimes, I called Sally to share my pressures; other times, I jogged in place. More and more often, I could recognize the beginning stages of my anger. My rested, peaceful soul rejoiced in the Lord and I knew Sally's prayers—and mine—were being answered.

During Bible study the following Monday, I sensed the Lord prompting me to ask the other ladies to pray for me and for the solution to my anger. *But, Lord, I don't need any more prayer. Sally is praying for me and I've been doing fantastic. Everything's okay now.*

But the urging continued even though I tried to ignore it. At the end of the Bible study, when Sally asked if there were any prayer requests, I blurted out, "Yes, I have one."

Feeling my face redden, I frantically tried to think of something else for which I could ask prayer. When my mind went blank, I stared at Sally. She smiled reassuringly.

*Okay, Lord, if you want me to, I will.*

Taking a deep breath, but speaking only slightly more than a whisper, I made my request. "Well, I wanted to ask . . . uh . . . to ask all of you to pray for me and . . . uh . . . my anger toward Sandy. I've been getting awfully angry at her lately and I'm having a hard time coping."

Julie giggled. "Oh, come on, Kathy, you're the last person who needs prayer for that. You're always so calm and cool with Sandy and Jeff."

"Yes, Kathy," Mary continued, "I'm sure it can't be that bad. We all get upset with our kids—everybody does. I'm sure you're making a big thing out of nothing."

Frustrated, I looked around trying to formulate my thoughts into words. "No, really, I need your prayers. It's been pretty tough these past few months, and I'm scared. I can't seem to grasp the Lord's power in this area of my life. Sandy gets to me too easily."

By now, everyone's sober faces had riveted on me. Julie spoke first. "I'm really sorry I laughed, Kathy. I just didn't take you seriously at first. But I'll remember to pray for you every day. I know that the Lord will strengthen you."

"Thank you, Julie. I really appreciate everyone's prayers."

The tension in my chest subsided as the seven women nodded their heads, agreeing to pray for me.

After Sally dismissed us, I felt awkward walking with everyone to the sitter's house. Then Julie spoke up again. "Kathy, I've discovered that if I don't try to repress my anger when I first feel it, I can face it and deal with it better. Repressing it only makes it fester within me."

"Yes, I agree," Mary joined in. "I've also heard that we should communicate our anger through 'I' messages instead of 'you' messages."

"Oh yeah?" I turned to Mary. "What does that mean?"

"Well, 'I' messages are phrases like, 'I feel angry when that happens.' Whereas, 'you' messages are words that imply blame like, 'You make me angry.' If I explain how I feel instead of blaming the other person, that person is less likely to become defensive about what I'm saying. And I have opened the door for better understanding and acceptance of my anger."

I nodded my head. I didn't completely understand all that she meant but I was beginning to see that there was a lot I needed to learn.

Then some other members of the Bible study, Pat and Anne, shared times when they had been angry with their children and I could see they were really trying to help.

*The Lord did want me to share my experience. He is going to use everyone's prayers.*

When we reached the babysitter's house, I opened the door and saw Sandy playing on the floor with blocks. She saw me and raced to me, hugging my legs. Full of hope, I lifted her into the air and kissed her. "Sandy," I whispered, "I love you and from now on things are going to be great."

# 12.

## Celebrate!

**June 20th.** "Honey, this is a really nice restaurant," I commented. "I'm so glad we came here."

"I thought you would enjoy it. After all, it's not every·
day we get to celebrate our seventh anniversary. Happy
anniversary!" Larry raised his water goblet into the air. I
lifted mine to meet his, gently clinking them together in a
toast.

Seven years before, on June 20, 1970, we were married.
But at this moment, I could hardly believe it. I scanned the
restaurant noticing the antiques and old-fashioned decor
which enhanced the romantic and nostalgic atmosphere. I
watched Larry sitting across from me, peacefully enjoying
his gourmet dinner of crab. As I savored my prime rib, I
mused over the ten years since I had met Larry at a high
school water polo game.

"Do you know what the most significant part of our
history together is for me?" I reflected out loud. "It is how
the Lord used you in my life to bring me to him. If you
hadn't taken me to your church, I might not have heard
that Jesus wanted me to know him personally. Thank you,
honey."

Larry's grin caused a flood of emotions to well up within
me. It was the same easy-going smile I remembered from
our courting days that had made me feel so special. My
insecurity had thirsted for his love and acceptance. Imagine! A guy had actually accepted me just as I was. I began to

feel the joy of that stability and love again. Then I remembered it was seven years later and the familiar, tormenting loneliness of the present brought me back to reality.

*If Larry really loves me like he says he does, why doesn't he spend more time with me? Oh sure, it's easy for him to take me out for our anniversary, but what about the way he treats me on the other days of the year?*

The insecurity and loneliness I had experienced before I met Larry returned, and I started to believe that his love and devotion had never been real.

Larry broke into my thoughts. "Sweetie, you look so sad. What are you thinking about?"

Pushing my creamed peas around on my plate, I stammered, "Oh, I was just thinking about . . . uh . . . about how you met so many of my needs when we were dating."

"Well, don't I meet them now?" he laughed.

I tried to laugh. "Well, I *would* love for you to spend more time with me."

Larry's smile faded. "Oh, that again. I've told you I'm trying to gain financial security for our family and that means I need to work longer hours. Believe me, it'll pay off in the end. You'll see."

My chest tightened in the familiar way that helped me recognize tension and stress these days. "Sweetheart, I know you want to do that. But I would rather have you around than money. I want *you*."

Larry rolled his eyes upward. "You just don't understand. I've explained it to you before."

*Oh no, now we're going to argue on our anniversary night. Boy, did I say the wrong thing. How can I put my feelings into an "I" message?* But rather than risking the possibility of saying the wrong thing again, I desperately tried to talk about something else.

"Have you noticed Jeff is sitting up for a few seconds already?" I tried to giggle. "He's such a good baby. Hope he lives through Sandy's picking on him."

Larry's effort to laugh at the changed subject made me realize the argument had been dropped. We were at a truce again.

For the rest of the evening, we skirted the issue of Larry's long working hours. Instead, we talked about our birthdays which would be celebrated the following week and about the family birthday party my mother was planning for next Friday.

On Friday afternoon, I was excited about the party. Evidently, Sandy sensed the excitement too, because she wouldn't stay in bed for her nap.

"Sandy, we're going to be up late tonight at the birthday party. You've got to go to sleep," I explained.

I walked her back to her bedroom. "Mommy, I not tired. I want to play," she whined.

"Now, don't start whining," I commanded her, my voice rising. "Please, Sandy, try to sleep. You'll be happier tonight if you're not tired. Now, just lie there and try."

I walked out of her room sensing that my trust in God's plan was being eroded by worry. *Lord, if she doesn't sleep, she's going to be a brat tonight. I don't want to have to come home early. Father, please help her to go to sleep.*

I had barely walked into the kitchen and begun wiping the counter when Sandy appeared at the doorway again. I gasped. "Sandy, you aren't even trying. Now get back in your bed, right now!" My facial muscles contorted into a fierce scowl. Opening her eyes wide, she turned abruptly and ran into her bedroom crying.

*Oh, that girl. Why doesn't she cooperate? I just don't understand why she can't lie still in that bed for even one minute.*

Suddenly, the heat of the day and tension in my body swallowed my patience. I couldn't stand it. I rushed into the bedroom and undressed. Beads of sweat clung to my body. I quickly pulled my bathing suit on and ran out to the backyard. I felt like screaming.

I dove into the pool and the cool water cleansed my body of tension and frustration. As I swam several laps, my tears mingled with the water. *Jesus, Jesus, please make Sandy go to sleep. When she doesn't take a nap, she cries and whines. I want to have a good time at the party.*

I climbed onto an air mattress and floated peacefully under the cloudless, blue sky. Kicking gently, I guided the raft around the pool, trailing my hands in the refreshing, sparkling water.

My thoughts wandered back to Larry and our discussion at the restaurant. *Lord, why can't I just love and accept Larry as he is? I'm always trying to change him, but it doesn't do any good. I want him to spend more time with me. I want him to talk to me more, but my nagging only pushes him farther away. Jesus, I really believe you want to make him into your kind of man, but it's not happening.*

An inner voice rebuffed me. "My thoughts are not your thoughts, neither are your ways my ways. . . . For as the heavens are higher than the earth, so are my ways higher than your ways, and my thoughts than your thoughts."

*Yes, Lord, I know those verses from Isaiah 55, but you still aren't doing anything . . . maybe I'm in the way with all of my nagging. Is that it?*

He didn't have to answer me because I knew it was. No matter how hard I tried to have kind, loving communication, invariably negative, pessimistic nagging would win over.

*Lord, I just don't feel loved. I know you love me but . . . I* tried to clarify my thoughts . . . *but with the way I treat Sandy and Larry, I guess I find it hard to believe you can love me. Oh, I know about your unconditional love but I don't feel it.*

Tears trickled down my temples into my wet hair. *Father, I really do want to love Larry and Sandy unconditionally. I just don't seem to know how.*

I paused as if expecting a sermon on love. But instead, three words echoed in my head: "Show your love."

*Show my love . . . show my love.* The words ricocheted in my mind. I thought of many ways to demonstrate my love but set them aside one by one, hoping for an unusual, spectacular way. Then it occurred to me: *I'll have a surprise birthday party for Larry! I've never done that before. I'll show him how much I love him and he'll have to love me back. Yeah, he'll be so grateful that he'll have to spend more time with me. That's it!*

I paddled over to the side and jumped out of the pool.

Wrapping a towel around me, I breezed into the house and down the hall, formulating in my mind the list of people I would invite.

Passing Sandy's room, I glanced in, expecting to find her playing. I stopped. Sandy lay on her bed, surrounded by books . . . asleep.

*Praise you, Lord! Oh, Father, I really appreciate you doing that for me. You showed me your love, now I'm going to show Larry mine.*

# 13.

## Surprise Party

**June 25th.** "Yes, Claudia, that's right. The party will be this Saturday. I'm glad you received the invitation so soon and can come." I was relieved that Claudia had called to let me know her invitation had arrived safely. I hoped I hadn't forgotten anyone.

Claudia was curious. "Kathy, how are you going to make the party a surprise if you're having it at your house?"

"That's the best part. I had Jim ask Larry to play tennis with him that afternoon at 1:00. Everyone will arrive at our house at 2:30, and Jim will bring him back at 3:00. Doesn't that sound great? I'm so excited. You know, I've never done anything like this before. I sure hope it works."

"Well, it sounds foolproof to me. I just hope Larry feels like playing tennis that day."

"That's the least of my worries. Larry will play tennis any chance he gets. What he may not like, though, is coming home all sweaty and tired to find twenty people waiting for him."

"I bet he'll love it. Well, I've got to go but count on us to be there and if you need any help, let me know. 'Bye."

" 'Bye, Claudia. Thanks."

I hung up the phone smiling. *This is going to be so much fun. I just can't wait to see his face.* In my heart, I counted on this feat to make Larry love me more, but I wouldn't admit it to myself very often—it sounded too selfish.

During the next few days, Sandy really got on my nerves. I had so much to think about and organize, and she seemed to sense my tension, demanding even more attention from me than usual. As I tried to plan the menu, she wanted to play with modeling clay which I knew would make a big mess. But I also knew that saying no would only elicit persistent begging and possibly a temper tantrum. I was not prepared to handle that, so I relented.

In the meantime, my mind swirled with plans. *I'll make the cake on Friday night while Larry is at work. Sally can keep it at her house until Saturday. But where am I going to hide all the extra food and paper goods? I don't have enough cabinet space in the kitchen.*

I tried to think of all the other places in the house where Larry seldom looked, possible hiding places, and I decided which of those I could use. That made me more confident. I was determined to pull this surprise off, hoping it would make Larry appreciate me more.

On Saturday morning, I could barely sit still. I tried to keep busy by cleaning the house. But Sandy and Jeffrey, sensing my nervousness, whined and cried for attention all day.

*Sandy, please let me get the house clean,* I pleaded mentally. The house was beginning to look better and I hoped Larry hadn't noticed my unusually furious pace. Once he left at one o'clock, I would have to put the kids down for their naps, take all the food out, wrap his gift, and get the cake from Sally's house.

Internally, I felt as if I were a rubber band pulled taut to its limit. Nothing could go wrong. This party had to come off perfectly. Larry would have to love me for this one.

I flashed back to another surprise I had pulled on Larry when we were first dating in high school. After school one day, when I knew he was practicing with his water polo team at a nearby college, I drove over and walked right into the pool area waving at Larry. He turned crimson as all his friends teased him because girlfriends never went to practices. I watched from a nearby bench for about twenty minutes and was the only spectator around. I was delighted when his buddies needled him for several days after that. Boy, was that fun. Although after the incident was over Larry kept telling me I shouldn't do it again, I could tell by his smile that he halfway enjoyed the attention.

Larry's voice broke through my reverie. "Kathy, Jim's here. We're going now."

"Okay, have a good time," I cried out from the back bedroom. Little did he know what he would be coming home to. Now, it was time to get busy.

Picking up Jeff, I walked to his room. I checked his diaper and moaned. It was dirty. I had changed him just thirty minutes before so I could put him down for his nap without hassle. Taking the opportunity to review mentally my "To-Do" list, I pulled a clean diaper out of the drawer and changed him again.

Distracted by thoughts of all the things that still needed to be done, I nervously laid Jeff in his crib and shut the door. *Whew, that's one thing settled,* I sighed. But I was only two steps down the hall, when I heard Jeff start to cry. *That's funny. He usually goes right to sleep.*

I walked back into his room and checked his diaper pins but didn't find anything wrong. I laid him down again. He began to cry immediately. "No, Jeff, no. Please don't do this to me. Remember, you're my good baby. Now, go to sleep."

I closed the door, hoping that being out of his sight would stop his crying, but he continued at full volume. *If I get him up, I won't be able to do as much as I would otherwise. He's got to go to sleep.*

I decided to put Sandy down for her nap and wait to see if Jeff would stop crying. After I raced through reading a book to her, Sandy wiggled on top of her bed. "Mommy, can we swim later?"

"No, honey, we're going to have company this afternoon. Now, Mommy really needs you to help and go to sleep, okay?"

"Goody, goody. Who's coming over?"

"I don't have time to tell you right now. Sleep tight!"

I almost slammed the door as I hurried out of her room.

My heart sank as I heard Jeff still screaming. *I can't let him scream like that. It drives me crazy. Maybe I can rock him to sleep.*

While rocking him, I concentrated on all the things I still needed to do. *Oh no, it's 1:30. I've got to hurry.*

Jeff's alert eyes stared at me. "For God's sake, Jeff," I whispered, "go to sleep." I rocked faster. I was one blink away from tears as Sandy's door creaked open. Watching her disappear into the kitchen, I sighed, "All right, Lord, I'll just ignore her for now. It's more important that Jeff goes to sleep."

The rocking chair squeaked faster and I tried to sing but my throat was too tight. Finally after fifteen minutes, Jeff's heavy eyelids closed and I laid him carefully in his crib. *Don't come in now, Sandy. Just stay away.*

Tiptoeing out of the room, I practically ran down the hall wondering where Sandy could be. The minutes were fast disappearing and the guests would start to arrive soon.

I turned the corner of the kitchen. Gasping from shock, I stopped. Sandy sat on the kitchen carpet surrounded by hundreds of tiny pieces of modeling clay. *Oh no, why did I leave that out on the counter?*

In one stride, I stood towering over Sandy. "Oh, damn. Look what you've done! I've got too many things to do without having to clean up this mess."

I raised my hand and shot it down, slapping Sandy's cheek.

Sandy covered her face with her hands and screamed hysterically. *I don't care. She's caused me trouble just when I need all the help I can get. Now, nothing will be ready.*

I dropped to my knees, trying to scoop up the muted-gray, speckled pieces.

"Sandy, Sandy, can't you do anything right? I told you we're having company."

As I picked up the mess, the slapping sound echoed within me. Guilt replaced my anger. *Oh no, Father, I've done it again. I wanted everything to be perfect and now I've spoiled it. Look what I've done to Sandy.*

Sandy stared at me as tears continued to roll down her

cheeks. As I started to move toward her, she again covered her face. I took a deep breath, then let it out slowly.

"Sandy, I'm sorry. I'm really sorry. Mommy wants to get everything ready for the party and you made a mess. I shouldn't have gotten mad at you, though."

I gently pulled her hands down from her face and tried to smile. "C'mon now, please help me get ready, then we'll go over to Sally's house and get Daddy's cake."

Her face brightened. "Cake? Okay."

I looked at the red mark on her cheek that was fading to a dull blush. *Father, I promise never to touch Sandy again in anger. I'm sorry.*

Sniffing back my tears, I grasped Sandy's hand and we went to get the cake. Shortly after we had returned and I had just taken out the chips and dips, the guests started arriving. Several of the women helped me set out the food, and at 2:50, I stationed one of the men at the window to look for Jim's car.

At 3:05 he yelled, "Here they come."

Everyone took their preassigned places. They were smiling and giggling excitedly. And several kept whispering, "Shhh," making more noise than before.

Suddenly, I remembered the movie camera. I ran down the hall, retrieved the camera, and stood ready.

Larry opened the door. His T-shirt was clinging to his wet skin and his hair was disheveled. He looked tired.

Everyone shouted, "Surprise!" and started singing "Happy birthday to you . . ."

Larry blinked. He stood with his mouth open, his hand still on the doorknob. He stared as everyone broke into laughter.

Larry's wide-eyed amazement broke into a half-smile. "Oh no, I can't believe it. You've got to be kidding."

He stepped over to the nearest chair and plopped down. I laid my hand on his shoulder and kissed him. "Happy birthday, sweetheart. I love you."

"Oh, honey, this is fantastic. How did you ever do it?"

"Not very easily," I joked, knowing the price had been high.

Everyone surrounded Larry and congratulated him on

his twenty-eighth birthday. Screeching her delight, Sandy ran over and jumped on his lap.

*Father, thank you that everything went so well—except for my outburst at Sandy.* My heart was heavy. It wasn't the sweet victory I'd expected. It showed me I wasn't handling stress as well as I thought. I could see that the battle was yet to be won.

# 14.

# The Barbecue

**July 10th.** "Honey, I just have to thank you again for the wonderful surprise party. That was something else. You really did surprise me." Larry wrapped his arms around me, squeezing tightly.

"I was really excited planning it," I said, returning his smile. "Just wait until you see the movies of you walking in that door. You won't believe the amazed look on your face."

But Larry's appreciative words weren't what I really wanted. Had he spent more time with me this week? No! He had been just as consumed by his work as usual. What did I have to do to get his attention anyway? Kill myself?

When Agnes and Neil's invitation came in the mail a week later inviting us to a neighborhood barbecue, I thought, *this will be Larry's opportunity to show me how appreciative he is.*

"Larry, did you notice Agnes and Neil's invitation to their house for Saturday?" I anxiously inquired.

"Yes, I did. Unfortunately, I already told Fred I'd work to repay him for a time he worked for me. I'm really sad I have to miss the barbecue."

I turned away disappointed. *Now, Kathy, don't get upset. He didn't do it on purpose; it just happened. Don't blame him; it's not his fault.*

Even though I realized it wasn't his choice to work, I wanted to blame him.

When Saturday arrived, Larry got ready to leave. Walking over to me, he commented, "Honey, I am really sorry that I can't go to the barbecue with you. It sounds like a lot of fun and I would have enjoyed being with you and the kids."

I stared straight into his eyes. "Really, Larry? Do you mean that? You really would have gone if it hadn't been for your promise to Fred?"

Larry appeared surprised at my intensity. "Of course, Kathy. Don't you think I want to go?"

My mind raced. I didn't want to get into another argument. How could I share my feelings without complaining?

"Well, it's just that I miss you so much and it seems like—you'll notice, I said seems like—every time there is something to do, you have to work. I just wonder sometimes if you even want to be with me and the kids."

Larry's hazel eyes softened. "I'm sorry I give you that impression. But I assure you I really do want to be with you. As soon as we get on our feet financially, I'll have more time to spend with you. I promise."

For the first time, I believed him. He really did want to be with us. I decided I would stop complaining and trust his love for me from now on.

A couple of hours later, Sandy, Jeff, and I walked over to Agnes and Neil's backyard where several families mingled. Agnes had prepared four large salads and the barbecue coals were hot-white, ready to cook the hamburgers and hot dogs.

Several of the neighbors sat in groups visiting, while children ran back and forth chasing balls and playing with the dog.

"Wow, Agnes, this is really special. But I still can't believe you wouldn't let me bring any food."

Agnes grinned. "Well, we just wanted everyone to come, have a good time, and not worry about anything."

"That's really sweet of you. Looks like you've got a good turnout."

I scanned the back yard. Noticing Pat and Sally talking together, I walked over to them. Sandy trailed behind me, fearfully eyeing the dog, and Jeff took in the view as I balanced him on my hip.

Once Sandy became acquainted with the dog, she raced around with the other children. I watched her play. She looked so darling in her clean, green-and-white-checked shorts outfit. Her blonde, short hair actually looked as if it were starting to get thicker. She was growing up so fast.

When it was time to eat, I prepared our plates and sat down beside Ted, one of our neighbors. Moving over on the picnic bench to make room for us, he helped me set down the glasses of punch.

Sandy eagerly began eating her hot dog. All her running around had made her ravenously hungry.

Ted leaned toward Sandy, brushing her bangs back from her sweaty forehead. "Sandy, you're such a good little girl," he remarked.

Pride welled up within me. "Yes, Sandy is a good little girl. Although she does sometimes remind me of the little girl in the nursery rhyme who when she was good was very, very good, but when she was bad, she was horrid."

Ted laughed.

"Sandy's my special little girl." I hugged her, kissing her on the top of her head. The love I felt at that moment almost made tears come to my eyes. *I really do love you, Sandy*, I whispered in my mind.

But by the time I had thought the words, confusion and guilt surrounded the warm feelings of love and suffocated them. Guilt snickered, "How can you say you love her when you treat her so badly?" Confusion poked, "What kind of love hits and kicks and slaps and . . ."

Trying to divert my attention, I turned to Ted. "I hear you landed a new job. How's it going?"

As Ted raved about his higher paying position, my imagination continued its dialogue. *I'm trying. I'm trying. I do love Sandy.*

"When she's good," the voice answered back. "What kind of love is that?"

*Why do I hate her so much when she's naughty?* I probed. *Can love exist alongside hate?*

Then I remembered a concept I had learned many years before. Love is a choice for the highest good of the person.

*That's the answer. Love is a choice, not a feeling. I do love Sandy. I just have to learn to express my love in choices for her good.*

The condemning voices seemed to retreat. I remembered the many ways I had hurt Sandy and as Ted continued to talk about his new job, I reassured myself: *I am doing better. I'm not getting angry as often. God is working. I just have to continue to trust him. And that's that!*

Later that afternoon, several of the women and I sat around a picnic table talking. Mary, a friend from my Bible study, asked, "Kathy, how are you doing controlling your anger?"

"Well, uh," I forced a smile, but my face grew hot, "I have my ups and downs. I guess I have the hardest times when Sandy makes mistakes. She does so many dumb things."

"Kathy, I think that's because she's a child," Julie, another friend from Bible study, spoke up.

"Yeah, I know that," I replied, "but it's so aggravating."

"I agree, Kathy," Mary said. "I did something once that helped me along those lines. Using the information I found in a child development book, I made a list of everything a child Jeremy's age might do, like spill milk, or not pick up his toys, or not share—things like that. I put the list on the refrigerator and each time he did one of them, instead of getting angry, I would put a check beside it. That really helped me to remember that his immaturity caused him to act the way he did. He wasn't doing it on purpose."

Everyone murmured their approval.

"Wow, Mary, that's a great idea. I'm going to do that." I mentally made a note to make myself a list the first chance I got.

The conversation continued and Anne began saying how thrilled she was that she had finally potty trained her two-and-a-half-year-old daughter. She raved about how nice it was not to have to wash diapers or change her daughter.

Anne's news made me think about Sandy. It had been several months since I had put Sandy back in diapers. She was over two-and-a-half now, maybe she was ready. It sure would be nice to have to change only Jeff. And the summer months were supposed to be the easiest time to try because she'd be able to run around in just her training pants.

I went home from the barbecue trying to decide if I should try potty training Sandy again. "Well," I assured myself, "if she doesn't respond right away or if I can't handle it, I can always quit. I'm going to do it."

When I made a list of things Sandy could be expected to do, I added, "Have lots of potty training accidents."

The next day, I dressed Sandy only in her training pants and reintroduced her to the potty chair. I hoped this time would be successful.

# 15.

## Seven Steps

**August 1st.**  I glanced at the many rows of book racks and was amazed. This Christian bookstore had added a lot of books and items since I had last been there. How was I ever going to choose a book for Alice, my neighbor, to read in the hospital?

Then, a title in the family section caught my eye. Picking the book up, I read *Understanding the Male Temperament* by Tim LaHaye. I laughed. *Boy, could I stand to learn about Larry's temperament.* The more I looked through it, the more interested I became.

Maybe if I understood Larry, I wouldn't always be trying to change him. I decided I would buy it, along with something else for Alice.

When I finally found a book I thought she would enjoy, I paid for both, and drove home hoping Sandy and Jeff would cooperate and let me read later on.

When Sandy and Jeff both went down for their naps easily, I praised the Lord. Now I could start my book. Two hours later I was still reading and was amazed that Sandy and Jeff were still asleep. Fascinated, I read about the four different temperaments that Mr. LaHaye described. I identified Larry's temperament—and mine. *No wonder he reacts the way he does. And no wonder I react the way I do. I've always known Larry doesn't look at things the same way I do, but I've never understood why. Now I know.*

For the next couple of days, I read during every spare moment I had. I began to understand my melancholy temperament was based on perfectionism. For the first time, I acknowledged that I did tend to be a perfectionist. I had never recognized that in me before. Maybe these perfectionistic tendencies were what made me so impatient and demanding of Sandy. I decided to keep an eye on myself and see if it influenced the way I treated her.

Toward the end of the book, there was a section called "How to Cure Anger, Bitterness, or Resentment." I wondered if following its seven steps could help me. A spark of hope lit within my heart as I read the section. Was this the real reason the Lord had me buy this book?

Step number one was: "Face your anger as sin." I didn't know if I wanted to call my anger sin all the time. I knew that my anger was a habit in my life, a habit that often controlled me, taking over my thoughts and actions. That was wrong. *Okay, Father,* I prayed, *I'm going to start off on the right foot by telling you that I agree my anger habit is wrong, that it is sin. And I ask you to forgive me.*

All right, what was step two? "Confess every angry thought or deed as soon as it occurs." That was interesting. Maybe the cause of my anger was really internal—my thoughts and perceptions. I recalled the last few times in which I was out of control. Every time had started with not trusting the Lord for the circumstances I was in. Then I became worried or tense and these feelings turned into anger. *Lord, I ask you to help me recognize when I'm starting to think negatively or angrily.*

"Ask God to take away this angry pattern" was step three. *Okay, I will. Father, I ask you to take away my angry thought pattern. Even as I ask you, though, my faith is weak. How can I ask so simply for such a complicated thing? Please help my unbelief.*

Step four was: "Forgive the person who has caused your anger." Sandy! Larry! They were the two people with whom I was most often angry. But forgive *them*? I was the one who needed the forgiveness. I was the one who was in the wrong. But I knew that I didn't totally believe that. I

believed Larry didn't spend enough time with me or have
the right priorities. And Sandy demanded too much of my
time and energy—too much of me. I was bitter toward
them and that was at the root of my problem. I had never
been honest with myself because I knew as a Christian I
shouldn't be bitter.

*All right, Lord, I ask you to forgive me for my bitterness
and help me to forgive Sandy and Larry. I know you are
using them in my life to make me more of the godly woman
you want me to be. I just keep taking the mass of clay from
which I am molded off your potter's wheel. Help me to stay
there from now on.*

"Formally give thanks for anything that bothers you,"
spelled out number five. This was becoming ridiculous. It
might take all day to follow through on this step. Everything bothered me: Sandy's wet and dirty training pants,
raisins in the rug, Larry working long hours, the dripping
faucet . . .

As I mentally listed annoying situations, I realized
these were the circumstances that flamed my anger.
These were the potentially dangerous situations I needed
to be careful of.

I jumped up from the sofa and retrieved a piece of paper
and a pencil. I wrote them all down and tacked it beside
Sandy's list.

Returning to the couch, I read the sixth step, "Think
only good, wholesome, and positive thoughts." I knew this
would be difficult for me. I tended to look at the negative
side of things and found it hard to focus on God's joy when
circumstances weren't going my way. I wondered how I
could combat that. Then I remembered someone telling me
about a "blessings list" they had made. Maybe if I made a
list of blessings, I could refer to it when I was thinking
negatively.

Another list? This *was* getting to be ridiculous. But I
knew it could help so I started writing. Ten minutes later, I
was surprised at how many blessings I had thought of. My
heart felt bubbly with thanksgiving.

After I put my blessings list on the refrigerator, next to

the others, I picked up the book again. Step seven: "Repeat the above formula each time you are angry." Now I understood. This wasn't just a one time thing, it was a process. I should follow this whole formula, step by step, every time I became angry. I could see it was definitely going to be a challenge to put the steps into practice.

But I finished the section and decided I would give Mr. LaHaye's method a try, allowing the Lord to cure me of my dreaded "disease," anger, which I knew was eating my heart out and destroying my life.

But I wondered how I could make sure I followed the seven steps. I often said I was going to try something and then forgot all about it. Thinking of my other lists, I decided I'd copy the seven steps down on a card and tape it to the window above my kitchen sink. That way I could memorize them and be reminded to use them.

I found a large, lined card in my desk, wrote the steps down, and taped it on the window above my sink. *Oh, Lord, please help me follow them. And help me get back to disciplining Sandy consistently with the spoon. That helped me so much before. Maybe, if I am faithful to both of these projects, I really will see victory. Jesus, I've got to. I don't know how much longer I can go on like this without doing something really destructive. I'll depend on you to remind me often.*

At that moment, he told me what to do: "Put verses about anger throughout the house."

*That's a good idea, Lord.* I fished out more cards from the desk, wrote down verses on them, and taped them in prominent places in the rooms I went into most often.

Now when I washed the dishes or fixed meals, I read the seven steps again and again until I had memorized them.

When I led Sandy in the bathroom after a potty training accident, I studied the card on the mirror. "Let all bitterness and wrath and anger and clamour and slander be put away from you, along with all malice. And be kind to one another, tender-hearted, forgiving each other, just as God in Christ also has forgiven you" (Eph. 4:31–32).

In the kitchen, when I retrieved the spoon to discipline

Sandy, I saw, "Hatred stirs up strife; but love covers all transgressions" (Prov. 10:12).

In Sandy's room, I put, "A hot-tempered man stirs up strife; but the slow to anger pacifies contention" (Prov. 15:18).

When I noticed myself starting to think negatively or complain about my life, I would pick several blessings and praise God for them. The checkmarks were lining up rapidly beside Sandy's mistakes, but instead of becoming angry, I understood they were a part of her process of growth.

Everywhere I turned, God reminded me he could help me control my anger. Although the flame of hope was strong within me, I still had occasional, flickering doubts about the true possibility of victory.

# 16.

## Victory in Sight

**August 30th.** My blurry mind struggled to wake up. I focused my eyes on the clock and read 8:04. Snapping alert, I listened for the children but didn't hear a sound. Evidently, Sandy and Jeff weren't awake yet. I was surprised. Remembering today was Wednesday and I had a La Leche League meeting to go to at 9:30, I realized I needed to hurry.

As I dressd, I heard Sandy playing in her room and Jeff babbling in his crib. Even though I started to feel rushed, I was happy. The past two weeks had gone smoothly. By repeating the seven steps, I had been able to catch myself almost every time my anger had started to erupt.

Sandy ran into my bedroom. "Mommy, what we having for breakfast?"

"Oatmeal and toast," I replied, putting on my sandals.

"I want pancakes. Pancakes, please, Mommy."

"No, Sandy, we had pancakes yesterday. I don't want you to have too much syrup."

Sandy's face puckered up into a tearless cry.

Rushing past her into Jeff's room, I began dressing him. I heard Sandy screaming in my bedroom; my chest and throat tightened. *Oh, Lord, I don't need her to have a temper tantrum when we're in a hurry. But step number five says to give thanks for anything that bothers me, so thank you that Sandy is having a fit.* I smiled. *This is almost comical. Here I am changing Jeff's dirty diaper and being grateful that Sandy is screaming in the next room.*

Jeff lay on his back on the changing table sucking his fist. His round, chubby belly wiggled as I wiped off his bottom. Suddenly, the phone rang. I picked up Jeff's naked body and raced to answer it. It was Claudia asking for a ride to the La Leche League meeting. I assured her I could be at her house at 9:15. When she continued to talk, I sighed helplessly. How could I tactfully get her to hang up? But within a few minutes she finished. I hung up the phone and noticed it was 8:30.

By the time we ate breakfast and I dressed Sandy, it was 9:00. I hadn't even packed Jeff's diaper bag yet. My tension increased as Sandy asked question after question, and to make things worse, I couldn't find my keys.

When I had finally packed the bag and found my keys, I was perspiring and gritting my teeth. I strapped Jeff into his car seat and reached for Sandy. I felt something wet. *Oh, no, it can't be. Not now, when we're late.*

"Sandy, are your pants wet?" Her frightened face stared at me. "You've been doing so well. Why did you pick this morning to have an accident?"

I gripped her arm tightly and pulled her into the house. Her little legs struggled to keep up. "Honest to God, Sandy, why now? Are you doing this on purpose?"

My tension turned to fury. "Now we'll be late and Claudia is waiting for us." I continued to spew out my frustration.

As I grappled to pull down Sandy's training pants, I noticed the verse on the mirror. "Let all bitterness and wrath . . ." *I don't care about that. She's doing this on purpose. She's got to be. She's been doing so well the last couple of weeks.*

I was jumping up and down inside. Tension-building thoughts raced through my mind: *I'm going to be late . . . Claudia is waiting . . .* I jerked my hand back and let it slam against Sandy's wet bottom.

"Next time you better tell me first," I yelled. By the time I had spanked Sandy five times, shame replaced my anger.

I escaped into Sandy's room searching for another pair of training pants. Returning to the bathroom, I sensed guilt and failure overwhelming me. "See, Sandy, that's what happens when you wet your pants," I defended myself. But inside, I cried out, *Oh no, I've done it again. I can't believe it. I've been doing so well and now I've blown it!*

I picked up Sandy and carried her out to the car. Tears tumbled down my face as I drove the car out of the garage. *Dear Jesus, I'm so ashamed. When am I ever going to learn? When am I ever going to get complete control? Do I have to practice the seven steps again?*

At first, I didn't want to go through them, then I remembered how much I had learned in the last couple of weeks. If I ignored my outbursts, I didn't have the Holy Spirit's power to resist becoming angry the next time. But when I followed the seven steps, I sensed a renewing, cleansing power that enabled me to control myself during the next aggravating situation.

*All right, Lord, here I go again. Father, I confess my outburst and spanking Sandy in anger as sin. I ask you to forgive me and to cleanse me even though I don't deserve it.*

I turned to Sandy but couldn't look into her eyes. Embarrassed, I asked, "Sandy, will you forgive me for getting angry with you?"

Sandy's tear-stained face gazed at me uncomprehendingly. I knew she didn't know what forgive meant but I needed to ask for her forgiveness anyway. Many times in the past weeks, I had consciously not become angry so that I wouldn't have to ask for her forgiveness.

Focusing on the Lord again, I prayed, *Jesus, I forgive Sandy for having an accident. Help me to remember that she doesn't do it on purpose, that she's still learning. Thank you that Sandy's accidents are helping me control my anger habit. It seems like it's taking a long time but I know I'm in the process of learning, too.*

I looked into the rearview mirror to wipe my face. Then I wiped off Sandy's. We pulled into Claudia's driveway and she got into the car with her two-month-old daughter.

Hoping I didn't look too upset, I tried, but found it hard to share Claudia's excitement over her daughter's latest accomplishments.

When we arrived at the park where our August meeting is always held, I hurriedly set out the books and items I sold as treasurer. The meeting began. I sat down on a blanket with Sandy in my lap and Jeff lying next to me. As a regular part of the meeting everyone shared stories about their month and this time most of the women talked about how great they thought it was to be a mother.

Guilt plundered my heart of peace and joy. It screamed within me, *What a terrible mother you are. You beat your kid and nobody else does.*

*No, no,* I argued. *God has forgiven me. He's forgotten about it and I'm cleansed.*

*How can you call yourself a Christian the way you act?*

*I'm not perfect, but Jesus is my Savior.*

When it was my turn to share, I mumbled something about how Jeff was starting to eat different kinds of foods. But all the while I wondered, *Don't any of them get angry sometimes? Will I ever have complete victory? Does God still love me even though I've failed him? Why don't I experience the joys of motherhood?*

After everyone had shared, Sandy played with the other children while I sold books and baby food grinders. It was close to lunchtime when I dropped Claudia off at her house. Sandy whined complaints about being hungry, but I tried to tune them out.

*Think positive! Think positive!* I began singing "Jesus Loves Me" and Sandy joined in. With a sigh of relief, I drove into our garage, unloaded everyone and everything into the house, and promptly fixed lunch.

As I thought about the morning, I tried to encourage myself. *I failed, but at least I'm not failing as often. Most of the time I'm able to catch myself before I'm out of control. I guess it's just going to take more time.*

In the next month, I coped with stressful situations better than I ever had before. When Jeff came down with another cold and was coughing throughout the nights, I napped every afternoon and regularly reviewed the seven steps.

Then I came down with Jeff's cold. Although my body was weak and easily irritated, I monitored my thoughts carefully to prevent negative thinking from capturing my mind.

I continued to discipline Sandy consistently with the spoon, and eventually, her misbehavior was slightly reduced. Her third birthday was coming soon, so I hoped she was growing out of the "terrible twos."

Little by little, like grains of sand dropping through an hourglass, I was seeing victory mount up in a pile. God was working, and for the first time I knew that some day I was going to be in control of my anger. Now when people complimented me on my patience with Sandy in public, I could smile and say "thank you" instead of mentally rejecting their praise. Maybe I wasn't such a bad mother after all.

# 17.

# Loved

**September 15th.** Picking up the phone, I answered, "Hello."

The woman's voice on the other end of the line asked, "Is Kathy Miller home, please?"

"This is she."

"Kathy, this is Joy from the Christian Women's Club. We've noticed how regularly you come to the monthly luncheons and wonder whether you'd consider serving as Nursery Chairman on our new board that begins in October. We'd really love to have you serve the Lord with us."

Surprised, I inquired, "What would the position entail?"

"It means you would attend the luncheons to collect the money for the babysitters, and also come to the two other board meetings we have each month."

"Oh, I see." I was flattered that they wanted me to join their board but I knew I couldn't agree to that kind of a commitment with all the other things I had to do. I also knew what Larry would say if I took on another responsibility.

"Well," I answered, "I'm really glad you thought of me. But . . . uh, I really don't think I could at this time. My son, who is only nine months old, is still nursing so it's hard for me to leave him for very long. And I'm an officer in an

organization called La Leche League which takes some of
my time. So I don't think I could. But I really do appreciate
you asking me. I enjoy the luncheons so much and you
women certainly do a great job of putting it together.''

Joy's disappointed voice replied, ''I'm sorry that it won't
work out now, but do keep us in mind for the future.''

We said goodbye and hung up.

I smiled as I thought about Joy's offer. It would be exciting to be involved in something that brings women closer
to Christ. But I really did have too much to do already and
it would be hard on Jeff to leave him so often. Even though
he was eating more solid foods, he was not ready to wean
yet. Besides, I wanted to continue being treasurer for La
Leche League for at least another year. I enjoyed it so
much. No, it just wasn't the right time.

The peace in my heart confirmed my decision. But within a few days, the thought of joining the board resurfaced
in my mind. I began to think about how great it would be to
work with a group of Christian women. But no, I decided it
just wasn't possible right now.

It was easy to bury the idea in the "not now, maybe next
year" cubbyhole of my mind as I thought about the responsibilities of my family, La Leche League, Bible study, and
maintaining my patience. I didn't need any new pressures
to undermine my control. I was sailing along fairly well
now, seldom losing control. I didn't want anything to com-
plicate my life.

But as soon as I thought the idea had been safely stashed
away, it reappeared. And like a woman falling in love with
a man she used to dislike, it became more attractive each
time it emerged.

In the following week, my desire to continue as treasurer
for La Leche League dwindled. I had enjoyed the role for
two-and-a-half years and now my love for it was slowly
disappearing. I was amazed. Each time I thought about the
board position, I became excited and drawn to the idea.
This was silly, I told myself. I had already told them no.
Most likely they had already found someone else. I tried to
forget about the possibility.

That Friday, while my friend Karen was visiting with her two children, the phone rang. It was a woman who introduced herself as Virginia. She was from the same Christian Women's Club.

"Kathy, we on the nominating committee were wondering if by any chance you'd thought any more about joining us as Nursery Chairman. The Lord hasn't filled that position yet. Is he keeping it open for you?"

Unable to restrain myself, I giggled. "Well, as a matter of fact, I have been thinking about it but I assumed the position would be filled already. I don't know what to say. Can I call you back in a few days after I've prayed about it and have talked with my husband?"

She agreed that would be just fine and left me her number.

My heart raced with joy as I hung up the phone and explained to Karen what had happened. She laughed. "It sure looks like the Lord wants you to join the board, doesn't it?"

"Boy, it sure does. But I don't know what Larry will say. He always says I have enough to do. Even if I quit the treasurer's job, the board position requires more time and responsibility. And what about Jeff? How can I leave him?"

"Well," Karen smiled. "If the Lord wants you to do it, he'll show you the way."

The rest of the day I felt excited, yet a little apprehensive, about talking with Larry. How could I ask him in such a way that he might say yes? *Lord, you're going to have to work with me on this one.*

The next morning after Larry finished breakfast, I sat at the table with him. I explained how both Joy and Virginia had called and asked me to be on the board, and how I had increasingly sensed the Lord changing my desires from the treasurer's job to the board position.

Taking a deep breath, I asked, "Honey, what do you think about me joining the board as Nursery Chairman?"

He stared at the hanging tiffany-styled lamp above us. Barely breathing, I waited and prayed, *Lord, guide him according to your will. I really want to join the board . . . please.*

He turned to me. "You really think this is what the Lord wants you to do?"

"Yes, I do. I was so sure I would stay treasurer for quite a while longer but he's certainly changed my desires."

"Then I guess that it will be all right with me."

Bursting with joy, I clapped my hands. *Thank you, Jesus, thank you. You want me to do it.*

"Larry," I grinned and kissed him, "I'm so glad you said that. I'm so excited."

I immediately reached for the phone on the wall. My hand shook as I dialed Virginia's number, but the happiness she expressed after hearing my answer was reassuring.

Then I called my La Leche League leader to let her know I would be resigning as treasurer. She said she was sorry to hear it but told me not to worry. There were several women who were interested, so she knew it wouldn't be difficult to find a replacement for the position.

For the rest of the day, I anticipated how my first board meeting would go. October fifth was only two weeks away.

During the next week, I prepared the treasurer's books for the new treasurer of La Leche League. As I finished totaling some figures, my pen ran out of ink. I stared at it in amazement. *This is the pen I've been using for the two-and-a-half years I've been treasurer. How interesting that it should run out of ink the last time I write with it as treasurer.*

The following week, Jeff suddenly started to balk at nursing. I couldn't imagine why he wouldn't nurse. His gums were bothering him a little from teething, but I didn't think that would prevent him from nursing altogether. He was becoming a lot more interested in food and he loved drinking from a cup, but I had expected him to nurse at least as long as I had nursed Sandy—fifteen months. However, each time I tried to nurse Jeff, he refused. I was incredulous!

One day as I stood at the kitchen sink washing the dishes, an understanding of all that was happening broke through to my soul like the sun bursting through the clouds after a storm. *Why, of course! With Jeff no longer nursing, I'll be able to attend the board meetings and not worry about him being hungry. And my pen running out of ink . . . it all means God is guiding me.*

*Thank you, Jesus. You are doing all this for me, aren't you? I can't believe it. You're showing me over and over again that you are specifically leading me. Your hand is directly upon me. Even though I've hurt Sandy and I'm not in complete control yet, you still love me. I'm important to you and you accept me as I am.*

Tears brimmed in my eyes, then plopped into the sudsy dishwater. The realization of God's love for me was overwhelming. "God loves me . . . again!" I cried out loud, hesitantly mouthing the word "again."

He had never stopped loving me, but the light of that fact had been dissipated in my heart by the anger and low self-esteem I had been nurturing. But now the full strength of that light dispersed all the gloom.

*I love you, Lord. I love you so very much!* Astonished, I paused in thought. *I haven't told God I love him for so long. It's been such a long time since I've felt loved by him and felt loving toward him. But now I want to shout it from the rooftops. God has shown me how much he loves me and I love him, too! He wants me to serve him; he wants to guide me; he wants to love me!*

I couldn't wipe the joyous smile off my face for a week— and I didn't want to. Sandy's temper tantrums didn't bother me. *God loves me!* Jeff's teething fussiness didn't phase me. *God cares for me!* The messy house didn't overwhelm me. *God is guiding me!*

Larry couldn't believe the change he saw in me. When he asked why I was so happy, I exclaimed, "Honey, God loves me. He's shown me how much he loves me!"

Larry's quizzical look didn't dilute my joy. "But I thought you knew he loved you!"

"Yes, but I had lost the joy of his love, of realizing he specifically loves me and cares about my life. He has

guided me to join the board. Everything that has happened—you allowing me to join the board, my pen running out of ink, Jeff suddenly weaning himself—it all
points to God moving in my life. I'm important to him."

Larry laughed. "Well, I'm glad it has meant so much to
you. That's great!"

Oh, it was great! I sensed that a new chapter was beginning in my life. A chapter entitled "God loves me and so
do I!"

# 18.

## Not Perfect Yet

**October 15th.** *Three years old. I can't believe it.* Sandy turned three on October twelfth. I smiled at her sitting on the floor watching TV. *Oh, Father, thank you for this last month. It has been glorious. I've rarely been out of control, but more importantly, I love you and I love myself. I know now that I'll never go back to my old angry habit.*

I looked again at my list of things to do in preparation for the family birthday party we were having for Sandy that night. I was relieved that it was a Saturday so Larry could be here and help me. As soon as he came home from his real estate appointment, he could set up the tables and chairs and stay with the kids while I did some last-minute shopping.

Suddenly, I remembered I forgot to tell him I needed his help that afternoon. But I was sure that he didn't have anything else to do so I expected him home sometime around one o'clock.

As I stirred the cake mix, I glanced at the clock. "Okay, Sandy," I called, "it's ten o'clock, time to turn off the television. That's enough cartoons for this morning."

She frowned. "Mommy, can I watch TV longer, please?"

*Well, she's the birthday girl so maybe she can. Oh wait, when I've let her watch TV longer in the past, it's been*

*twice as hard to get her to turn it off the next day. No, it'll
be better if I remain firm on my rule.*

"No, sweetie. There are lots of other things you can do.
Why not get out the new toys you got from your birthday
party the other day? Your new dolly will be lots of fun to
play with."

Pouting, Sandy dramatically turned off the television. I
stifled a laugh. She would be a good actress some day.

After she skipped down the hall toward her bedroom, I
finished the cake and put it into the oven. I wished I had
done more things the day before, but my battle with the flu
had made me weak. I looked around and decided I still
needed to clean the range, mop the bathroom floor, dust,
and vacuum.

I retrieved the vacuum from the hall closet and passed
Jeffrey crawling toward his yarn ball. "Hey, Jeff, you're
really going to town with your crawling, aren't you?"
Reaching down, I picked up the soft, multicolored yarn
ball and tossed it out in front of him. With a squeal, he
crawled toward it.

The phone rang. It was my sister asking for some ideas
for a birthday gift for Sandy. Then we started talking about
other things and before I knew it, twenty minutes had
passed.

Hanging up the phone, I dashed down the hall, looking
in each room for Sandy and Jeff. I finally found Sandy
enthralled in front of the television set watching cartoons.
Jeff sat nearby trying to stack blocks. I pushed the off but-
ton. Startled, Sandy looked up and started to cry.

"Sandy, I told you, no more television."

I turned on my heels and fetched the vacuum again.
Quickly plugging it in, I began vacuuming in the living
room. In the adjacent family room, I could see Sandy
pounding her fists on the floor. Icy chills traveled down
my back and my chest muscles tensed.

*When are these temper tantrums ever going to stop? I
thought she'd be over the "terrible twos" by now. Thank
heaven the tantrums don't come as often as they used to.*

I tried to ignore her and thankfully remembered Larry would be home soon.

By the time I finished vacuuming the rest of the house, it was 11:30. Walking toward the family room to check on Sandy, I heard the TV.

*Again! Won't that girl ever learn?* I had had just about enough of this. She was going to learn once and for all. The icy chills I had sensed before blazed into hot flames of wrath.

Passing through the kitchen, I noticed the card with the seven steps tacked on the window. I stopped, took a deep breath, and exhaled slowly. *All right, Kathy, calm down. Yes, Sandy disobeyed but she's only a little girl. You're not perfect yet and neither is she. Your anger is not going to make her obey. Jesus still has to discipline you and you will have to continue to discipline Sandy. So you might as well get used to it.*

I pulled the wooden spoon out of the drawer. Moving toward Sandy, I prayed, "Lord, thank you for reminding me. Thank you that you're smoothing Sandy's and my rough edges so that we might become beautiful diamonds sparkling to the praise of your glory."

I turned off the television. As soon as Sandy saw the spoon, her mouth dropped open. "No more TV, Mommy. I promise. No spanking, please?"

"Yes, Sandy, I do have to spank you so that you'll remember next time not to turn on the television."

After swatting Sandy on her bottom three times, I cuddled her as we talked about how important it was for her to obey me. Then we started talking about her birthday party. She quickly recovered from her crying and her face brightened at the prospect of cake and gifts.

"Sandy," I pleaded, "Mommy really needs your help. I have a lot to do to get ready for your party. Can you play nicely while I dust, and then it will be time for lunch, okay?"

Sandy nodded. She jumped off my lap and ran into her room. I heard her fishing several toys out of her overflowing toy box.

Feeling relieved, I put Jeff in his playpen and dusted the living room furniture. As I thought about all the other projects I had wanted to accomplish that day, I grimaced. I was just going to have to settle for whatever I could get done. It wouldn't matter that much if the house wasn't spotless.

I reminded myself about the perfectionistic tendencies I was discovering within me. I had been recognizing my "all or nothing" attitude: If everything wasn't done, I couldn't be satisfied. Now I was learning to be content with whatever I could accomplish. It was just as pleasing and less stressful.

Sighing in resignation, I finished dusting the bedrooms and heard my stomach rumble with hunger. It was time for lunch.

We finished lunch without hassle and by 1:30, Sandy and Jeffrey were asleep for their naps. Sitting near the front window, I expected to see Larry's car drive up at any moment. I decided to read a magazine since Larry would be home soon. I finished reading an article, but he still had not returned. Finally, I decided that I needed to get back to work, even if Larry wasn't home yet.

As I took my china out of the cupboard, I found myself fuming inside, *Now, why is he late? He must know we have a lot to do to get ready for the party. I can't set up that heavy table all by myself. Where is he?*

My anticipation evolved into anger during the next hour. Realizing that stress was choking out my trust in the Lord's timing, I often paused to quote some verses on anger. I sensed temporary relief and thanked the Lord. But when Larry still didn't arrive, the tension returned.

*Father, please make him come home soon. There is too much for me to do alone. And please help me with this anger I feel. I've really been trying to control my emotions. And I don't want to make Larry feel guilty when he comes home. Right now, I submit to your plan and timetable for today. I thank you that you are in control and that I can trust you. Everything that you want to get done will get done.*

I felt peace wash away my anger and tension. It was so
exciting to see the Lord helping me again. It seemed that
his immediate peace was always available as soon as I
relaxed in his control. I had experienced it happening over
and over again.

Suddenly, I heard the sound of the garage door moving
and the hum of the car. "Lord, thank you that you're helping me to have the right attitude."

Larry rushed into the bedroom where I was doing some
last-minute chores. "Hi, Kathy. I'm sorry I'm late but I
went by Bob's for a minute. He's still pretty sick even
though he's doing a little better now. He might be able to
come back to work in about a month."

I expected my anger to return but instead, I sensed the
peace within as strongly as I had felt it before. "I'm so glad
he's doing better," I replied. "That was thoughtful of you
to visit him."

"I've been meaning to get over to see him for a long time
and decided I better do it today and stop putting it off."

Setting his keys down on top of the bureau, he turned to
face me. His dark hair and hazel eyes appeared especially
handsome to me.

He grasped my hands and pulled me down with him
onto the bed. "You know what? I sure do appreciate you."
He wrapped his arms around me.

I tried to pout but giggled instead. "You do, huh? I don't
know if I appreciate you. I wanted you to come right home
so that you could help me get everything ready for the
birthday party tonight."

Larry began to pull away his arms but I held them
around me.

"It's my fault, don't worry," I interjected. "I didn't tell
you. I thought you would realize it. Don't get me wrong.
Now I'm glad you went to see Bob, but I sure was getting
angry with you when you were late."

"Honey, I can't read your mind. You've got to tell me,
otherwise I don't know. Of course I'll help you." He started
to sit up but I pulled him back.

"Larry," I paused, clarifying my thoughts, "I realize that

I do expect you to be a mind reader. I'm always thinking you should automatically know my needs and then meet them. I've got to start sharing them with you."

"So start now." Larry gazed intently into my eyes.

I diverted my eyes from his and smoothed back his hair from his forehead. "Well, I guess one of my needs these days is for more attention. Unfortunately when I've tried to tell you that in the past, I haven't been able to do it without making you feel guilty for being gone so much." I stared into his eyes. "So let me change my appeal a little by requesting that we talk more when you're home. Maybe somehow we can have more time to communicate and air our feelings. Sometimes I feel so alone. With everyone else's husbands home in the evenings, I really start to feel cheated."

"Kathy, I can understand how that could happen. From now on we'll try to talk more. Maybe we won't turn on the television so soon after the kids have gone to bed. How does that sound?"

"That would be fantastic!" I leaned over and kissed him.

I jumped up from the bed laughing. "And now I request we get ready for Sandy's third birthday party. Let's go!"

Grabbing his arm, I pulled him up in mock strength. After I told him what things still needed to be done, I left to finish my shopping.

That evening, Sandy had a great time at her birthday party. Everything wasn't perfect like I had intended, but she didn't notice and neither did anyone else. But more important to me was my calm and peaceful attitude. I wasn't perfect yet, but I had a handle on my anger. I was content and on my way to victory.

## 19.

## Forgiven

**November 15th.** Mother and I relaxed on my living room couch planning Thanksgiving dinner, which was only a week away. Sandy handed me her doll to dress and then brought in a game to play.

"Well, Kathy," my mother laughed, "you might as well find something we can all do together. Sandy doesn't want to be left out."

"Yeah, I guess you're right. At least it's not too long until her bedtime. Sandy, would you like us to play ball with you?" I reasoned that Mother and I would still be able to talk while rolling a ball back and forth.

"Yes, yes, let's play ball," Sandy cheered. She ran to her bedroom and returned with her red plastic ball.

"Sandy," I explained. "Grandma and I will roll it on the carpet and you can jump over it."

"Okay." Sandy's eyes brightened in delight.

I positioned myself on the floor, a few feet away from my mother. We rolled the ball back and forth and continued to plan the dinner. Each time it rolled across, Sandy took careful aim and jumped over it.

"Now, what will we serve for dessert?" my mother asked.

"How about our customary pumpkin pie and . . ." I began. Then I gasped in horror as I saw Sandy jump on top of the ball. Her feet flew out from beneath her and with a sickening thud, the back of her head slammed down onto the carpet.

I froze.

Mother reached over and cradled Sandy's rigid body in her arms. A moment later, Sandy's body fell limp and her head dangled over my mother's arm.

"Oh no, Mother, she's unconscious," I yelled.

Mother started slapping Sandy's face, calling, "Sandy, Sandy, wake up."

I jumped to my feet. "I'm going to call the paramedics." I ran to the phone in the family room and picked up the receiver with my trembling hands.

"Kathy," my mother shouted, "Sandy's conscious again."

I put the receiver back and ran to the living room. Sandy's eyes were open but she looked dazed. I knelt beside her and cupped her face in my hands. "Sandy, how do you feel?"

Her eyes tried to focus on me and her head wobbled in my hands. "My head hurts." She lifted her hand to touch her head.

"Okay, honey. It's bound to hurt considering how hard you hit it." I took her in my arms and sat down on the couch.

Mother and I sat there for a while discussing what we should do. Soon, Sandy complained, "Mommy, my tummy feels sick. I want to go to sleep."

I tried to smile but my lips felt heavy. "That's the first time in her whole life she's volunteered to go to sleep. Mother, I'm going to call our clinic and see what they say."

I lifted Sandy into my mother's lap. When I reached the nurse on the phone, I told her what had happened. She suggested I take Sandy to the nearest emergency room. Then I dialed Larry at work and he said he could meet me at the hospital.

Mother stayed with Jeff and within minutes I carried sleeping Sandy into the hospital. After I filled out insurance forms, the nurse escorted us to a bed surrounded by white curtains. The room smelled antiseptic.

Dr. Monning walked up to me and introduced himself. He asked me several questions and then explained that they would need to take a skull x-ray. A few minutes later, a man in a white uniform gently lifted Sandy onto a small rolling bed and wheeled her into another room.

It seemed like hours later when the technician brought Sandy back. She was still asleep and looked so little in the big bed. Her peaceful face appeared angelic and innocent.

"Oh Sandy, I hope you're going to be all right." I caught myself. *No, that's not true. I don't want you to be all right. I wonder if I would really be that sad if you died. Sometimes I think I hate you. I long to be freed of the responsibilities and burdens of being a mother.* I stopped. *I'm not supposed to feel this way,* I rebuked myself. But I knew I couldn't hold these feelings in any longer. I let my thoughts continue.

*I wanted to have a child so much, Sandy. We tried for three years before you were finally conceived, and now I wonder whether I want you around at all. You demand so much from me. Sometimes I want to be free.*

I felt ashamed, but at the same time, it was as if a heavy burden were being lifted off my heart. I was finally being honest with myself. Tears welled in my eyes.

*Sandy, I haven't hurt you for a long time and I'm not going to again . . . but I still resent you. You seem to want more from me than I am able to give. I'm trying to trust God for the future but I wonder if I've hurt you permanently, psychologically. I read somewhere that children who have been abused usually grow up to abuse their own children.*

*Oh, Heavenly Father, I don't want that to happen. Please protect Sandy. Please keep her safe from such a future. You know I never wanted to hurt her. You know I'm sorry. Please forgive me and heal Sandy's inner wounds.*

I stared at Sandy. Pulling a handkerchief out of my purse, I wiped my cheeks and blew my nose.

"Kathy, how is she doing?"

Larry's voice startled me. I stood up, turned around, and reached for his hand. "The doctor hasn't said anything yet. Oh, I'm so glad you're here."

A few minutes later, Dr. Monning joined us. "Mr. and Mrs. Miller, Sandy has a concussion but she's going to be just fine. The skull X-rays show there isn't any damage. You can take her home, just keep an eye on her for the next twenty-four hours. Wake her up through the night every four hours or so, and feel free to call me if you notice anything wrong."

The next day, Sandy played as hard as ever. I watched her and was particularly aware of her bright smile and loving vivaciousness. I began to realize how much I would have missed these moments if anything had happened to her. The realization became stronger as the day progressed and I felt a stirring of love in my heart for her. I knew that I didn't hate her and the sensation of God's forgiveness cleansed my heart.

That night as I tucked her into bed, I stroked her bangs back from her forehead. Love for her overwhelmed me. I wanted to cry with relief.

*Sandy, I do love you. I didn't think I did, but the Lord has shown me how much I really do. It still hurts me to think of how I used to hurt you, but I'm going to trust the Lord to heal that hurt. In the meantime, I know that he has forgiven me.*

I kissed her forehead. "Good night, Sandy. Sleep tight." I walked to the door and turned off the light.

"Mommy, I love you," Sandy called.

I turned to face her in the dark. "Oh, Sandy, I love you very much and I'm glad I can say that and mean it now. Good night, honey."

# 20.

## In Control

**December 3rd.** November stepped aside to make room for a festive December. It was hard to believe Christmas would soon be here. Christmas decorations draped the streets and almost every television commercial advertised some new toy or gift. Sandy grew more excited each day thinking that all the toys, dolls, and miscellaneous trinkets were going to be hers.

November had meant celebrating Thanksgiving. But for me every day was a thanksgiving, a giving of thanks and praise to the Lord who was delivering me from my anger.

At the December Christian Women's Club board meeting, Joy announced plans for the board's Christmas party. It was to be a formal evening for couples and sounded exciting. But when she informed us it would be on Tuesday night, December twentieth, I felt disappointment fill my heart—Larry worked on Tuesday nights.

When I mentioned the party to Larry the next day, his saddened face disclosed it would be impossible for him to take the night off. But somehow, an unexpected peace grew within my heart as I calmly told him, "Sweetheart, I'm sure that if the Lord wants you to go with me, he'll somehow find a way for it to happen."

Larry's skeptical frown almost pricked my ballooning hope, but I reminded myself of Proverbs 3:5–6 which I had been trying to keep at the center of my thoughts for the last week. "Trust in the Lord with all your heart and do not lean on your own understanding. In all your ways acknowledge him, and he will make your paths straight." Even if it meant going to the party by myself, I was determined to trust the Lord and not get uptight.

As Christmas drew closer, Jeff became increasingly fussy with teething. Just when he had started sleeping consistently through the night, I was once again being awakened by his pained cries.

One Wednesday around midnight, Jeff's squall invaded my dream. In a fogged haze of weariness, I pulled myself out of bed and made my way to his room.

Picking him up out of his crib, I soothed, "Oh, Jeff, are your teeth hurting again? You are really having a hard time with them, aren't you? Let's go get some aspirin."

After giving him the aspirin, I laid him on my shoulder and sleepily sank down into the rocking chair. As it squeaked softly amidst the silent, cool night air, I prayed, *Dear Lord, help Jeff's gums stop hurting now so that he and I can get back to sleep.*

The placidity enveloped me and my mind and heart absorbed the loveliness of the moment. Even though my body yearned for the warmth of my bed, my spirit longed to praise the Lord.

*Oh, Father, you are doing such marvelous things in my life. I stand in awe at your power . . . and your forgiveness. Lord, you've forgiven me so many times and yet I know you'll have to forgive me many more times.* I smiled. *But at least not as often as before.*

I still experienced eruptions of anger and frustration, but it wasn't unbridled anger anymore. I was in control. Life was beautiful and Jesus had never seemed so real. My devotions took on a new luster, like the sparkling Christmas ornaments around me. I loved working on the Christian Women's Club board. The Lord used me there and I had a purpose for living. Even though my marriage wasn't exactly the way I wanted it to be, I believed the Lord was going to make it a lot better one day. I just had to wait for his timing. For right now, I was content to continue accepting Larry as he was and to work on greater patience and joy.

I was loved and that love was flowing onto Sandy. I still battled anger, frustration, and stress, but instead of believing that I was losing the battle, I knew I had won the war. Victory was mine to claim. Life was challenging and exciting.

The impact of my reverie cascaded onto my soul like a waterfall streaming down rocks into a clear, sparkling pool. My heart burst with thanksgiving and joy. "Lord, you have delivered me. I'm not a child abuser any longer. I am free," I whispered.

Tears trickled down my cheeks and I hugged Jeff tighter. I kissed his head. *Thank you, Jesus. Thank you. I'm so grateful. I love you so much. Thank you for loving me during this past year even when I didn't deserve it. The joy I'm experiencing in this moment is worth the wait of all those months.*

Without realizing it, a song began to form on my lips. "Turn your eyes upon Jesus, look full in his wonderful face. And the things of earth will grow strangely dim in the light of his glory and grace."

*Oh Jesus, yes, your glory and grace wipe out all the pain and sorrow of this year. You've touched me. I love you.*

Many songs filled my mind as my joy sought expression. Jeff was asleep but I wasn't concerned that I might wake him. I wanted to wake the whole world. I wanted everyone to know: Jesus was in control of my life!

The next couple of days were filled with shopping, baking, and sending out Christmas cards. Christmas was approaching all too fast; and Christmas dinner at my home for ten family members was foremost in my thoughts and plans. I hadn't had time to even think about the board's Christmas party.

Then unexpectedly one day, Larry said, "You'll never guess what my boss told me last night. I have too many vacation hours on the books and have to take some time off before the new year. Isn't that wild?"

I jerked my head toward him. "Honey," I exclaimed,

"that's the answer to my prayer. Now you can go to the board Christmas party. Can you ask for next Tuesday, the twentieth, off?"

He smiled. "Yeah, that's right. That's great! Sure I can. Now, they'll have to let me have it off."

I could barely sit still as I grinned at him. *Thank you, Jesus, you did it. I trusted you and you did it."*

Larry's smile grew as I hugged him. "Kathy," he replied, "the Lord has rewarded your faith. I wasn't sure he could do it but he did."

My excitement grew all that week after Larry confirmed he could have the night off.

On Tuesday evening, we arrived at the fancy restaurant of a local hotel. I was truly grateful that Larry was beside me as we ate the delicious food and enjoyed the special entertainment.

Five days later, on Christmas morning, Sandy woke us early. She was so excited about seeing what Santa Claus had brought her. Instructing her to stay in her room, Larry, my mother, and I turned on the Christmas tree lights and made sure the camera was ready to capture her delight as she reacted to her presents. I opened the drapes. The dawn's soft pink light filtered into the room creating a fairyland effect on the presents and the tree. The blinking lights of the tree cast red, blue, and orange shadows on the walls and my spirit was illuminated with hope and joy.

Christmas morning . . . the day we celebrate our Savior's birth and the first step in his journey for our salvation. And this was the morning of the birth of a life free from hurting Sandy, free from uncontrolled anger, free from condemnation and hate. As a cocoon opens to reveal a ready-to-fly butterfly, my life was opening also—opening to love, self-esteem, faith, and patience. Christmas morning . . . the beginning of salvation for mankind and the beginning of an abundant life for me.

# Epilogue

Two months later, from February tenth through the twelfth, God performed the miracle that I had been trusting him for—the healing of my marriage.

On that particular weekend, Larry and I attended a marriage-encounter seminar that revitalized our relationship and reassured me that Larry did truly love me afterall. I learned that all my doubts and fears about his love were unfounded. And we were reunited in a oneness that we hadn't experienced since the early days of our marriage. What had been a fragile thread of communication between us became a steel cable.

As a bonus, my self-esteem was raised even higher as I experienced God's love and forgiveness in an even greater way than I had before. After that precious weekend, Larry and I became involved in the seminar's volunteer organization and two years later, the Lord directed us to become involved in Christian Marriage Communication which presents a similar kind of weekend seminar. Our unity grows as we serve the Lord in that ministry.

In the ensuing years, I've seen God continue to teach me more about dealing with anger, frustration, and stress. Being the kind of mother I want to be is still a difficult, conscious choice of demonstrating unconditional love and spending quality time with Sandy and Jeff. But little by little, that choice becomes easier.

I'm trusting the Lord, and seeing his miracles work in my relationship with Sandy. The Lord has healed our relationship and now we're good friends in addition to being mother and daughter. One of my strongest desires is to accept her always as she is—independent and strong-willed—because, in the past, I wasn't able to do that. Now, through God's grace I can.

Being a parent is definitely one of the most difficult jobs on earth. And of all jobs, it has the most at stake—the life of a unique individual. Happy is the parent who believes God's promise that "children are a gift of the Lord; the fruit of the womb is a reward" (Ps. 127:3). Patience and understanding may require focusing on the pleasant times that we have experienced with our children, and we can comfort ourselves with the knowledge that we are sharing in the tremendous joy of seeing a human being mature before our eyes.

As I see my children grow, I am learning to give myself credit for the times when I am a "good" mother and to forgive myself when I fail. I'm also growing in my ability to live in the power of the Holy Spirit, moment by moment.

When my anger was out of control, I thought that what I experienced could never be used for good or for God's glory. But God is a creative God. He can work all things for good. Now I experience a deep satisfaction and an inexpressible joy as I see God work through me to minister to others.

To God belongs all praise and glory.

# Appendix

Almost one million cases of child abuse were reported in the United States in 1982. Yet, experts believe that there may be as many as 6 million actual child abuse incidents occuring yearly.

The United States Congress defines child abuse as the "physical or mental injury, sexual abuse, negligent treatment or maltreatment of a child under the age of eighteen by a person who is responsible for the child's welfare."

I would add that the behavior must be recurrent in order for it to be labeled abuse. In other words, I would not call occasionally striking or spanking a child *abuse*. But I would identify someone like myself, who repeatedly lost emotional control and acted out of anger, as a child abuser.

Child abuse is found in many forms. Parents Anonymous, a self-help, crisis intervention organization that helps parents prevent child abuse, lists six different types of abuse.
*   physical abuse
*   physical neglect
*   sexual abuse
*   verbal abuse
*   emotional abuse
*   emotional neglect
You can see that even *neglect* is considered a form of child abuse.

Studies show that the average age of an abusing mother is twenty-six and the average age of a battered child is four (with most abused children being younger than two).

But what causes child abuse to occur? There are a number of

contributing factors. Evidence reveals that in many cases abusive parents:

- have been abused themselves as children (although this is not true in my case).
- are socially isolated and rarely have time away from their children.
- have experienced a series of changes or crises and, as a result, feel depressed, lonely, and/or fearful.
- demonstrate an inability to cope with stress.
- receive little support from other family members.
- have troubled relationships with their spouses.
- lack knowledge about child development and effective discipline.
- hold a negative attitude toward their victim.
- suffer from low self-esteem.
- have perfectionistic tendencies which lead to unrealistic expectations for self and child.

Researchers have also found that a child's crying is the behavior that most upsets abusive parents. And problems associated with toilet training are second. When a parent cannot successfully quiet or potty train a child, anxiety and frustration build and anger often surfaces.

Psychologist H. Norman Wright defines anger as a strong emotion of displeasure that often results from frustration or from having a goal blocked. People frequently equate anger with losing control, and many Christians call that sin. I agree that if we lose control, the uncontrolled behavior is sin and should be confessed.

But on my road to victory over anger, I discovered that learning to distinguish between the attitude of anger and the feeling of anger gave me more control over my actions.

You see, if we call all anger wrong, then we are apt to repress all angry feelings lest we sin. But doing that will only make us more angry because anger that is buried alive usually resurfaces later.

Instead, we can recognize that the first flash of anger within us is a feeling (not an attitude) of anger that is neither right or wrong. A feeling flares up within us; we have little control over it. This is different from an attitude of anger, which results from a decision not to deal with the feeling. Not recognizing, confronting, or dealing with an angry feeling can prevent understanding of it, which, in turn, can lead to long-term resentment, bitterness, or rage.

Ephesians 4:26–27 states, "If you are angry, don't sin by nursing your grudge. Don't let the sun go down with you still angry— get over it quickly; for when you are angry you give a mighty foothold to the devil."

I believe this verse emphasizes my point. It implies that we are going to get angry, and anger isn't wrong as long as we deal with it. It's what we do with our feeling of anger that determines whether or not we will sin.

Once we feel the first flash of anger, we can react in three ways. We can deny, direct, or declare the emotion.

Denying the anger is a destructive way of dealing with it. This action only causes the anger to be repressed. Ignoring anger does not make it go away.

A second way of dealing with anger, directing it, can be either healthy or destructive. If we use the energy that is stimulated by anger to accomplish tasks like cleaning the house or pulling weeds, but fail to examine the cause of our anger and take action to control the emotion, then we are directing our anger in an unhealthy, destructive way. However, if we first direct the anger but cope with it after the initial surge of energy has subsided, then we are reacting in a healthy, positive manner.

I think the third possible reaction to anger that I mention is the best: declaring anger in a constructive way. We want to accept responsibility for our anger and react in such a way that we demonstrate full awareness and control of our emotions. It is important to communicate our angry feelings with an honest, yet loving approach.

Let me share a four-step process that will help us react to anger in healthy ways.

The first step is to *realize* angry feelings. We can do that by being aware of our red flag warnings, those feelings we have before we reach the point of losing control and blowing our cool.

For instance, fifteen minutes before I explode, usually I am worried about a time schedule or upset about some other pressure. At ten minutes before, I feel tense and hurried, and my chest muscles feel tight. When I'm gritting my teeth and raising my voice in quick, terse commands, I know my five-minute warning is signaling.

If we can get in the habit of acknowledging our own unique red-flag warnings, we'll be able to recognize when our fifteen

minute countdown has begun and we can proceed to the second step.

The second step is to *magnetize* our mind away from our anger, and the physical tension and increased energy it often causes, with a distractor. A distractor, any activity that helps us turn our attention away from our anger, is used to allow a brief cooling down period and relieve the anger before it is negatively directed toward another person.

Here are a few possible distractors:
- take a vigorous walk
- run in place
- hit a pillow or a punching bag
- take a shower (with or without screaming)
- sing loudly
- take ten slow, deep breaths and count them out loud
- play a musical instrument
- recite an uplifting Bible verse
- telephone a friend, a hotline, or a professional counselor

The third step is to *recognize* the underlying cause of our anger. In many cases, when the situation is examined closely, we find that the immediate circumstances are not the real causes of our anger. Instead, we realize that we have focused our anger away from the real cause and toward a readily available, but perhaps inappropriate, target.

When trying to determine the actual cause of my anger, I find it helpful to have a mental checklist of possible causes.
- *Physical.* Am I tired? Do I need some exercise?
- *Psychological.* Am I thinking negatively about something? Am I worried? Is some relationship troubling me? Are my expectations for myself unrealistic?
- *Spiritual.* Am I not trusting God? Do I have some unconfessed sin?

Once the actual cause has been determined, we can move on to the fourth step which is to *verbalize* our anger in an appropriate way.

We can do this by using "I" messages instead of "you" messages. "I" messages express feelings and opinions—they reveal needs—without expecting the other person to change and without telling the other person what to do (unless that person asks how he or she can help). "You" messages like, "You make me angry," or "You shouldn't do that," accuse and often provoke a negative reaction. Although it is difficult not to blame or have expectations of the person to whom our anger is directed, we can find strength by trusting God for the circumstances of our lives.

Another way to safely and constructively express our anger is to write down our negative thoughts and feelings. Many times this will be enough to release the anger. But if not, it can be a good way to prepare for sharing our anger in a calm way.

If we'll go through this four-step process each time we get angry, we'll make sure that we control our anger instead of letting it control us. Remember, "Anger doesn't kill people or relationships. But stifled anger does."

When trying to understand and control anger in our lives, we must consider stress. Each one of us is under a tremendous amount of stress, and stress in itself is not wrong. It is when we allow stress to overpower us in such a way that we react negatively, when stress becomes distress, that we are in danger of becoming out of control.

What is stress? Stress can be defined as any condition or situation that imposes demands for change upon us. Did you know that we are even under stress when we are sleeping? No one is ever without stress. It is a part of every aspect of our lives. We can even look upon stress as positive because it can strengthen our relationship with God as we turn to him for help. However, it is important to recognize when stress becomes distress in our lives, because it's likely we are not trusting God in that situation.

What are some causes of stress? First, there are expectations—what we expect of ourselves, what we think others expect of us, and what we think God expects of us.

Without realizing it, my melancholy temperament had led me to expect perfection from myself all my life. And each time I didn't meet that unrealistic standard, my self-esteem took a beating.

When I became a Christian, this problem increased. After all, didn't I have the power of God to make me holy and perfect? Didn't God command me to be holy as he is holy?

And when I became a mother, I thought I should always be happy with my baby and never be upset with her. I feared that any sign of my displeasure would destroy her self-image.

These issues tore down my self-esteem as I saw how imperfect I was. Now slowly, I am accepting the fact that no one is perfect; we are all in a process of growth. We do not have the ability to make ourselves perfect; only Jesus can do that. Besides, in God's eyes, I am already perfect because I am covered with Jesus' blood and forgiven. Now I'm learning to become more like Christ in my daily walk of faith, but I realize I will never reach perfection here on earth.

Not only what we expect of ourselves, but what we think others expect of us can be stressful. When I couldn't control my anger toward Sandy, I didn't want to tell any one because I didn't want my image as a mature Christian woman to be destroyed. In addition, I thought confessing my sin would somehow stain God's reputation. After all, if I was having trouble, didn't that mean God wasn't powerful enough to help me, or others?

Now I know that I shouldn't live my life by what others think of me or expect from me. I should live my life under God's rule. Understanding this has freed me to let others know when I'm hurting so they can pray for me and help me. I realize that usually others don't judge me as harshly as I judge myself. And we can benefit from the help of those who care.

But what about God? Doesn't he have expectations of us? Yes, he does. But even though he has called us to be holy as he is holy, he also realizes we are in a process of growth. Only Jesus is perfect. No one else has been or ever will be. He knows that. God is not surprised or shocked when it takes us a while to gain victory in a problem area of our lives. It is important for us to understand that he doesn't get upset or condemn us when we sin, because if we think he does, we will try to rationalize, excuse, or justify our sin in some way. Instead, God wants us to ask forgiveness and go on living in the power of the Holy Spirit.

Another stressful factor in our lives is worry. When we worry, our thoughts are most often concerned with the past or the future, not the present. So we worry in vain because worrying can't help the future or change the past.

Here are three strategies to help us cope with worry. First, when we start to worry, we can think of the worst possible thing that could happen. Then we can think of reasons why the situation we're worried about wouldn't be so terrible after all. You see, worry is rooted in the vagueness of a situation. But if we go ahead and think of the situation's conclusion, often the thing we thought we feared doesn't seem so bad after all.

Second, we can claim Romans 8:28: "And we know that God causes all things to work together for good to those who love God, to those who are called according to his purpose."

We can let go of our worry because God is in control of our lives if we allow him to be. If he lets what we fear happen, it means he has a better plan. Remembering how much he loves us will help us realize he'll use that plan for our good.

The third strategy for coping with worry is not to take on a responsibility that God doesn't intend for us to have. I have discovered that when I'm worried about something I think my husband should be doing, I am trying to assume the responsibility for him. But doing that causes anxiety and fear in me and doesn't allow God to work in my husband's life because I'm in the way—and I'm usually nagging.

The last cause of stress I'll mention is allowing ourselves to become too busy. This is a real temptation for Christians because we see how valuable and necessary so many Christian projects are. And people like me, who have a hard time saying "No," think that if they don't do it personally, the job won't get done. Remember, "A need is not necessarily a call."

It is also important as we deal with stress to make sure we are filled and empowered by the Holy Spirit. Although Christians are indwelt by the Holy Spirit from the moment of their salvation, they may not necessarily be controlled by him unless they submit to him. We can do that simply by asking him to fill us and by making moment by moment decisions to let him control our lives.

I like to use a visual aid that helps me remember the Spirit is in control of my life. When I am starting to feel pressured or angry, I take a deep breath and envision the Holy Spirit entering the center of my life. Then I exhale slowly and try to visualize all my tension and anger flowing out of my body. As I continue to take several deep breaths and exhale slowly after each, I focus on the sense of the Spirit within me, helping me handle my current problem.

Anger, stress, and abusive actions don't have to be a part of our lives. I encourage you to reach out for the help you need if anger is a problem for you. Seek someone with whom you feel comfortable sharing your problem, preferably a professional Christian counselor. And keep in mind that God is always there with you. He wants to offer you the help and hope that you need. He came to my rescue. I know that he can help you, too.

If you would like to write me, please do so at:

P.O. Box 1058
Placentia, CA 92670

God loves you. So do I.